the

Ukulele

owner's

manual

Publisher: David A. Lusterman

Editor: Blair Jackson

Managing Editor: Kevin Owens

Design and Production: Joey Lusterman

Cover Photograph: Joey Lusterman (Spalted-Mango Romero Creations Replica Ukulele)

This book was produced by String Letter Publishing, Inc.

941 Marina Way S., Suite E, Richmond, CA 94804

(510) 215-0010; stringletter.com

ISBN 978-1-936604-42-5

CONTENTS

Chapters with this icon ▶ have accompanying video.
To access these videos, please visit **store.UkuleleMagazine.com/UOM**.

SHARING THAT JOYFUL SOUND

BY JAKE SHIMABUKURO

When I was four years old, my mother put an ukulele in my hands, and it changed my life forever. She taught me a simple chord, and the sound of my little fingers strumming those four strings brought me so much joy. But never in my wildest dreams did I ever think that I would be traveling the world someday with the opportunity to share that joyful sound with concert goers and music lovers.

As a kid, I didn't have many hobbies—I just loved playing the ukulele. I would practice all the time. In fact, my parents would have to take the instrument away from me so that I would do my homework, eat dinner, and go to bed.

Growing up in Hawaii, I was very fortunate to be surrounded by the ukulele, as it was a big part of the local culture. The ukulele was basically a hybrid of two Portuguese instruments that were brought over to the Islands over a hundred years ago: the machete and rajão. But it didn't take long for the instrument to develop its own unique personality, which is a big part of its wide appeal. Recently, more and more people have taken an interest in the ukulele, causing a tremendous rise in instrument sales. It makes a lot of sense, because the ukulele is affordable and not intimidating. Every year, more ukulele makers are advertising their new instruments and publishers have been releasing more ukulele sheet music and instructional content. And, of course, the whole online world has opened new doors for the instrument and its players.

A few years ago, when I first came across *Ukulele* magazine, I was completely blown away. For the first time in my life, I was able to read through an entire magazine where every page and article spoke to my heart. It was like a dream. In Japan, the word *otaku* means "maniac." And I was indeed an ukulele *otaku* who had found his ukulele guidebook for life.

I am so thrilled with the release of this compilation of articles from various issues of *Ukulele*, and as an avid fan of the magazine, I'm excited to read the new, additional content that is included. This book is truly a gift for all ukulele enthusiasts.

Let's all keep spreading the joy with this wonderful instrument that brings people together. And remember, if everyone played the ukulele, the world would be a better place!

CATCH THE WAVE!

Welcome to the Golden Age of Ukulele! I know what you're thinking: "Wasn't the Golden Age of Ukulele from the teens to the 1930s?" Well, yes and no. It's true that near the end of the 19th century and during the first two decades of the 20th century the Hawaiian-born ukulele was introduced to millions of Americans though a series of World's Fairs and expositions in Chicago, Portland, Seattle, and, most famously, the 1915 Panama-Pacific International Exposition in San Francisco. Hawaiian music entertainers (musicians and dancers) toured successfully in the U.S., ukuleles imported from Hawaii became popular with a small niche of enthusiasts, and the instrument started being built

by American companies, including Harmony and Martin. Not coincidentally, the uke's initial rise coincided with widespread sales of phonographs and records, followed in the early 1920s by the broad adoption of radio and, just a few years down the line, "talking pictures." This was the instrument's "First Wave," which crested during the fabled Jazz Age, but ebbed during the Great Depression.

The "Second Wave" came in the early 1950s with the arrival and incredible success of the new medium of television. Thanks in large part to entertainer Arthur Godfrey and his ceaseless promotion of the little four-string on his popular TV program, the uke enjoyed renewed popularity with a

whole new generation, particularly kids this time 'round. The combination of Hawaii becoming a state in 1959, and Elvis Presley shooting such films as *Blue Hawaii* (1961) and *Girls, Girls, Girls* (1962) in the Islands extended the Second Wave a bit, though it never achieved the sort of penetration in the national consciousness that it had during the First Wave.

It's fair to say that in both the First and Second Waves, the ukulele was regarded more as a fad than as some sort of lasting member of the great musical family—a curiosity rather than a serious instrument; indeed, it was often marketed as a toy.

It could plausibly be argued that *artistically* speaking, the uke took its greatest strides during the 1970s and early '80s, when Eddie Kamae and other great Hawaiian players of that era's neo-traditionalist revival redefined the instrument's role and inspired so many players that followed. But that was mostly in Hawaii—the Hawaiian folk renaissance never enjoyed much popularity, nor exerted much influence, on the American mainland or around the world.

It's hard to pinpoint exactly when the current Third Wave began, but there was a confluence of events in the early 1990s that provided considerable momentum to the ukulele's latest—and greatest—rebirth.

Jim Beloff is widely credited as being one of the early driving forces of the Third Wave. In a tale that has taken on some of the mystical glow of Arthurian legend, in early 1992 Jim and his wife, Liz, stumbled upon a Martin tenor uke at the Rose Bowl flea market in Pasadena, California.

He became obsessed with the instrument and, as he puts it, "by the end of that year we published our first *Jumpin' Jim's Ukulele Favorites* songbook. The response to that book was significant, including an interview in March 1993 on NPR's *Morning Edition,* which was heard by a large national audience." That was followed by various TV interviews, and articles in the *New York Times, L.A. Times*, and other publications, all of which "contributed to the feeling that the ukulele was showing signs of life again." Many more books—including Beloff's seminal 1997 volume *The Ukulele: A Visual History*—followed, as well as DVDs and albums. More than any other player, he has been responsible for demonstrating the instrument's range and capabilities through his tireless advocacy.

It helped, too, that right around the time Jumpin' Jim was getting his business going, the uke world's first bona fide superstar emerged unexpectedly: Israel Kamakawiwo'ole, a gentle giant better known as "Bruddah Iz," became a global phenomenon through his amazingly evocative medley of "Over the Rainbow" and "What a Wonderful World," sung in a haunting high tenor, accompanying himself on soprano uke. It led to Iz's 1993 *Facing Future* album becoming the first million-seller of any Hawaiian record. It's appeared on many film and TV soundtracks, and has become a de facto modern standard.

Just as the first two Waves were aided by the rise of particular media—recordings, radio, film, and then television—the Third Wave has been helped immeasurably by the explosion of the internet beginning in the early '90s with the introduction of the World Wide Web, and really shifting into overdrive in 2005 and 2006 with the arrival of YouTube and Facebook. All of a sudden, ukulele players all over the world could connect and share their love of the instrument, offer lessons, shoot videos of themselves playing tunes, provide tips and opinions on buying or selling ukes; the impact is literally incalculable, it is so vast. It is not surprising, either, that it led to the formation of an untold number of ukulele clubs scattered around the planet, which in turn has helped precipitate an explosion of ukulele festivals and destination-workshops from coast to coast in the U.S. and practically every country in the world (no lie—even New Guinea!).

YouTube has created a number of star teachers and performers, none bigger than Jake Shimabukuro, whose electrifying virtuoso performance of George Harrison's "While My Guitar Gently Weeps," went viral around the world (more than 17 million views to date!) and made the ukulele unquestionably "cool" to thousands of emerging players. Harrison, too, had a role in the Third Wave boom when footage of him casually playing the uke was included in *The Beatles Anthology* multi-part 1995 documentary series. As Beloff says, "Here was the lead guitarist of the greatest rock 'n' roll band in history, showing serious love for the 'jumping flea.'" Beatles songs are a vital part of the modern uke repertoire; you'd be hard-pressed to find a play-along event where a Fab Four tune doesn't turn up! But cruise around the internet now and you'll find ukulele performances in every style imaginable, from rock to jazz to country to classical to punk, and more.

The intense international interest in the ukulele has, not surprisingly, led to more and more instruments being made at every price-point and in every size. You can take your pick of tonewoods (or man-made materials, such as carbon fiber), add electronics, have a cutaway; they can be simple or incredibly ornate, custom-crafted or manufactured. Many players own multiple ukes, often in different sizes. There are more ukulele strings available than ever before, and smartphone apps by the dozens for everything from tuning to playing tips.

The *Ukulele Owner's Manual* is designed to help you better understand your ukulele(s). Drawing on the nine-year history of *Ukulele* magazine, as well as specially commissioned writings about the instrument, this illustrated guide offers wisdom from top players and teachers about a wide range of instrument-related topics, including the parts of the ukulele; the ukulele family tree; what to look for when buying a uke; a primer on strings; care and maintenance; traveling with your uke; cases and other accessories; and more—plus fun and informative chapters on the instrument's evolution, ukulele collectibles, and rare (and crazy) instruments.

We know how important your ukuleles are to you. So many players develop truly special relationships with their little musical companions. Well, the more you know about them, the more you will love them! We hope this guide will nurture that love.

—*Blair Jackson*
Editor, Ukulele *magazine*

A lineup of soprano, concert, tenor, and baritone ukuleles shows how the ukulele grew in size.

THE UKULELE FAMILY TREE

Sopranos, concerts, tenors, baritones, and more—the nut doesn't fall far from the tree

BY GREG OLWELL

From its humble beginnings as a child born to immigrants in Hawaii, the small soprano ukulele quickly became one of America's favorite instruments in the early decades of the 20th century. As the ukulele's popularity swelled, players and makers began changing the instrument, in the process creating an entire family that comes in many shapes and sizes. As its family tree expanded, the ukulele became more comfortable for some people, while also creating new sounds and looks that continue to thrill and delight today's players.

A big part of the ukulele's appeal is its simplicity. At its most basic, you could call it a small box—usually (but definitely not always) made from wood—that amplifies vibrating strings. Even on your first day playing a ukulele, it's relatively easy to make music with one, and for builders, the uke's elemental construction makes it a great jumping-off point for experimentation in shapes, sizes, materials, and nearly any design whimsy.

Here we'll take a look at the ukulele family tree and meet the members of the family, which come in four basic sizes—soprano, concert, tenor, and baritone. Well also meet a few of the family's more interesting relatives, which usually come in one of the established sizes, but can offer players different sounds. We'll start by looking at each size and uncover some history. Let's begin at the roots, with the original ukulele, the soprano.

Farida soprano

SOPRANO

The ukulele as we know it was born sometime after a ship of immigrants from the Portuguese island of Madeira arrived in Hawaii in 1879. This group included three people who are often credited with creating the ukulele: Augusto Dias, Jose do Espirito Santo, and Manuel Nunes. Though it's not clear that any member of this trio can lay claim to this singular invention, the ukulele is the result of combining the traits of two Madeiran stringed instruments: the small size of the *machete* with the tuning of its larger cousin, the five-string *rajão*. The ukulele quickly caught on, and after some experimentation, the soprano standardized to a tuning of G C E A (with a high-G) on a scale of 13-9/16 inches. The soprano's small body, coupled with its tuning, which features a higher-tuned string in place of what would normally be the lowest pitched string, gives the soprano a peppy, lively sound that can be immediately identified. Some contemporary players suggest that the soprano is only suitable for children or beginners, but it has found favor with some of today's finest players, who consider it to be the ukulele in its purest form. Nearly every maker offers a soprano, and the quality can range from custom-made professional instruments down to unplayable ukulele-shaped-objects (USOs). Not to be outdone by the small soprano, sopranino or pocket sopranos are even smaller playable versions of the soprano.

Enya concert

CONCERT

The concert is the next larger size and it is the most popular ukulele in today's market. The concert ukulele first appeared as players began asking for a louder, more comfortable instrument for bigger venues and more advanced music. The concert had its beginnings as a larger-bodied version of the soprano, called a taropatch, which used eight or sometimes four strings on a bigger, deeper body and a longer 15-inch scale to create more volume. Soon, people began requesting these larger versions only as a 4-string and the concert ukulele was born. It uses the same G C E A tuning as the soprano, and when paired with a larger body and longer scale, the concert ukulele produces more volume and a slightly deeper, rounder tone than the soprano. Nearly every maker offers concert ukes, and the size remains a favorite for people who want the ukulele sound on a slightly roomier instrument.

TENOR

You might notice a pattern with the tenor ukulele. In the ongoing quest for more tone and volume, the tenor ukulele employs the same G C E A tuning but adds a larger and deeper body than a concert, with a neck that stretches the scale length to 17 inches. This result is an instrument with even more room for fretting and picking hands and a deeper tone. The extra room is one reason why the tenor is the second most popular size today and the one favored by many professionals and enthusiasts. Nearly every maker offers a tenor, and since they're so common, there are a few makers who only offer tenors. Some tenor players replace the high-G string with a low G string in search of more harmonic and melodic range from the instrument, and while the change adds a few notes on the low end, some players feel that these low-G tenors have less of the ukulele's characteristic brightness. Many tenor players choose to use a strap because the tenor's larger size makes holding it a little more work and a strap helps to free up their arms up to make playing easier.

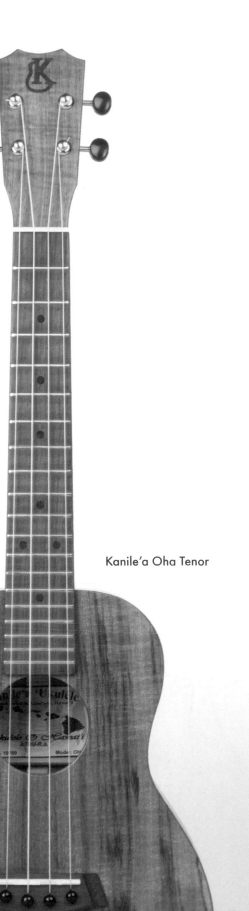

Kanile'a Oha Tenor

Ohana Baritone

BARITONE

The final—and largest—of the main four ukulele sizes to develop was the baritone. The baritone first appeared in the late 1940s and was designed by either Favilla or Vega—there is some debate about who was first. Baritone ukuleles usually have a scale between 19 and 21 inches, with a linear tuning (D G B E) that breaks from the ukulele's standard reentrant tuning with a high string on the low end of the fretboard, making baritones the most guitar-like ukulele. As the largest ukulele family member, the baritone has a deep, throaty tone and was a favorite of Arthur Godfrey, the popular 1950s TV personality who championed the ukulele during the instrument's second wave of popularity. Many guitar players who want to explore the ukulele appreciate its familiar tuning.

BASS

The newest member of the ukulele family is also the largest: the bass ukulele. The function of a bass ukulele is very similar to that of an electric bass guitar—produce a thundering low-end bass sound—but on a much smaller scale. The bass ukulele really took off after Kala began producing its U-Bass and people began discovering depths unheard from any ukulele before, while its portability made it a favorite of bass players looking for big tone in a small package. The bass uke uses a body roughly the size of a baritone, with a wider neck to accommodate four low-tuned strings. Unlike the other family members, the uke bass is meant to be played almost entirely using single notes plucked with fingers or soft pick instead of strummed. The ukulele bass shares its tuning (E A D G) with the larger bass guitar and uses very thick strings to achieve the low tuning on a short, 20–21-inch scale. Because the thick strings can't produce much volume acoustically, the basses are always fitted with electronics, which help the instrument be heard through an amp or PA system.

Kala Wanderer U•Bass

MULTI-STRINGED, BANJO, RESONATOR UKES & TIPLES

Breaking away from the size-based grouping of ukuleles, there are many variations to the classic ukulele, from instruments made from novel shapes to ukuleles that are, for all intents, ukulele versions of other instruments.

One of the first and most popular alternatives is the banjo-ukulele, which initially appeared around 1917 as ukulelemania first swept across the Mainland. Banjos were popular at the time, and it was natural to combine the neck and tuning of a ukulele with the circular head and body of a banjo. Also known as the banjolele, the banjo-uke helped meet the volume needs of vaudeville and concert hall performers, including George Formby, the British entertainer who turned his career as a popular singer of cheeky songs into film superstardom. Today, you can find banjo-ukuleles from Beansprout, Deering, Gold Tone, and Kala, among others, and they remain a popular choice for players looking for an instant vintage tone that will slice through the largest ensembles.

The quest for greater volume was common in the days before amplification and in the late-1920s, the National Stringed Instrument Co. created the resonator ukulele, which involves a mechanical form of amplification.

These distinctive instruments, like their resonator guitar brethren, are driven by a spun aluminum cone that acts much like a speaker cone in a home stereo, amplifying the sound of the strings. Perhaps the most dynamically responsive ukuleles, resonator ukes possess the ability to go from whisper-soft to cover-your-ears loud, depending on the force of your strumming hand.

Kala Banjo Ukulele

Gold Tone Reso Uke

The metal-bodied versions have a chiming, bell-like tone while wooden models have a rustic bark. Thanks to modern production techniques, resonator ukuleles are now more popular and accessible than ever, giving players options that range from affordable import models sold under brands like Kala, Gold Tone, and Sound Smith, to the modern National Reso-phonic company and custom makers like Morton and Ron Phillips.

Multi-string ukuleles are another way that makers found to increase the volume of early ukes, and because they make a richer and broader sound, they're most popular today for use in accompanying singers. As mentioned earlier, the taropatch was originally a larger-sized ukulele that eventually became the concert size, but you can also find 8-string versions in tenor and baritone sizes. They have eight strings that run in courses, or pairs, and are usually tuned in unison. Taropatches were more popular in the 1920s, but lost favor as larger ukes made the volume bump from the hard-to-tune taropatch obsolete. A 6-string tenor, which has two single courses and two double courses, was developed by Sam Kamaka, Jr. in 1959 and is sometimes known as the Liliu, in honor of Hawaii's last monarch, Queen Liliuokalani. Retro-crooner Casey MacGill favors a Morton 6-string tenor resonator ukulele for his swing-based music, while fleet-fingered phenom Taimane Gardner prefers a 5-string tenor, which has both a low-G and high-G, for her flamenco-inspired playing. The tiple (pronounced *tip-pull* or *tea-play*) is a 10-string instrument based on ukulele tuning, and with its steel strings it produces a jangly, bright sound reminiscent of a mandolin. Tiples have two unison courses on the outside and a tripled course, with a central string tuned an octave below the course's two other strings. They found favor with a few swinging vocal harmony groups in the 1930s and 1940s, including the Spirits of Rhythm and the Cats and the Fiddle. Martin pioneered the tiple in the late teens of the 20th century and produced them by special order until 1993, while Regal, Harmony, and Lyon & Healy also made them in the pre-World War II years. Ohana recently began offering an all-mahogany version. *u*

UKULELE TUNINGS

The soprano, concert, and tenor sizes all share the same tuning, but the different body sizes and scale lengths bring out different tonal qualities. Part of the ukulele's special sound comes from its use of reentrant tuning, G C E A, with a high-G, which differs from the linear, descending tunings found on most stringed instruments. The most popular modern tuning variation substitutes a low-G on a tenor (and occasionally on a concert), expanding the instrument's range. One variation that you might encounter is sometimes called Mainland tuning; it's a full-step higher, A D F# B, and is often seen on old sheet music.

The two largest ukulele family members have different tunings and are not reentrant like the smaller members. The baritone is pitched like the highest four strings of a guitar, making it a popular choice for wandering guitarists, and the bass ukulele, which while close in size to a baritone, uses special thick strings that gives the instrument a low pitch appropriate for playing bass lines.

SIZE	TUNING	SCALE LENGTH
Soprano	GCEA	13-9/16"
Concert	GCEA	15"
Tenor	GCEA	17"
Baritone	DGBE	20–21"
Bass	EADG	20-3/4"

UKULELE ANATOMY

Get to know the different parts of your ukulele

BY GREG OLWELL

Ukuleles come in several shapes and sizes, but they are all played using the same basic technique. A player picks, strums, or plucks the strings with one hand, while using the other hand to press down the strings to the fingerboard to make chords.

There are four primary sizes, from smallest to largest: soprano, concert, tenor, and baritone. You may also come across the bass ukulele, which has similar features but is a different instrument that uses a different technique. The four main ukuleles can all be played the same way and make music together equally well, with each size having a different feel and a different sound. It's worth trying them all to find one that is most comfortable to you. Many ukulele players own multiple instruments and often have ukes of different sizes.

The different sizes are based on the length of the string, or scale length, which is measured from the bridge to the nut. The longer scale instruments usually having a larger body and a sound that is deeper and darker. A longer scale-length means longer strings with more space between each fret. The scale length for each size is: soprano, 13-9/16 inches; concert, 15 inches; tenor, 17 inches; and baritone, 19 or 20 inches.

Ukuleles have two basic tunings, or pitches, you tune the strings to. Soprano, concert, and tenor ukuleles share the same tuning, G C E A, with the third string (C) as the lowest pitch. Some tenor and concert players prefer to extend the instrument's range by using a low G string, a variation called low-G tuning, to contrast with the standard, or high-G, tuning. The baritone uses a different tuning, D G B A, with the D as the lowest pitch.

BRIDGE

The bridge is attached to the top of the body and transmits the strings' vibrating energy to the body. The strings are anchored to the bridge, often with a knot, and pass over a thin strip of bone or plastic called a saddle.

SOUNDHOLE

Usually a circular opening in the top, the soundhole helps project the instrument's sound. The sound comes from the resonating body, and the hole's size and shape help to give the instrument its tone. Some ukuleles have a second hole on the side called a soundport, which directs sound up to the player. A decorative element around the soundhole is called a rosette and can range from a simple painted stripe to an elaborate inlay made from stained woods or shell.

STRINGS

Strings stretch from the bridge to the tuners and they are plucked, strummed, or picked to create sound. They are usually made of synthetic materials like nylon or fluorocarbon. Avoid metal strings on a ukulele; they are not built for the tension.

FINGERBOARD

Sometimes called a fretboard because of the metal frets inlaid along the fingerboard, this part is often made of rosewood or ebony. Frets divide the fingerboard into different notes. Small markers on the fingerboard and side of the neck help give players a visual clue for quick placement while playing. The nut is at the far end of the fingerboard and establishes the space between each string and the height above the frets.

TUNERS

The tuners, or tuning pegs, twist to bring the strings in tune. Some are geared, which can assist precise tuning, and others are friction tuners, which are held in place by friction.

HEADSTOCK

The headstock is at end of the neck and is where the tuners are attached. It often carries the brand's logo.

WHAT TO DO WHEN SHOPPING FOR A NEW UKE

Tips from two pros

I.
FIRST, SOME GENERALIZATIONS

BY SARAH MAISEL

I cannot stress how important it is to carefully choose your instrument. Once you've decided that you are ready to dedicate yourself to becoming a musician, you want to ensure you have the best instrument you can afford. I'm not saying that you need to buy a $2,000 ukulele, but you want to find the best one for you because this instrument will be your best friend, helping you through good times and bad.

Depending on where you live, this can be quite difficult. However, if you can take the time to diligently search, it will be worth it.

In my ukulele journey, the first uke I bought was a Flea. I adored that uke and it was perfect for getting me started (and for taking to the beach). Once I began to really get in deep with lessons, I realized that the instrument had limitations. I wanted to be able to play amplified and I found that the smaller size was a bit more difficult when trying to play jazzy chords. This led me to really think about what I wanted in my next instrument, and more importantly, the bigger issues that anyone can use when looking for a good match.

TRY THEM ALL OUT

Do not limit yourself on price when searching. This is a mistake most people make when they first start shopping, because they are either too scared to try the more expensive models or they don't feel they are "worthy" of such an instrument. Trying out all ukes, instead of shopping by price, will give you an idea of what specs are ideal on your instrument. You will learn things that you like and things that you don't like; then you can begin to narrow your choices down to an instrument that is closest to your ideal specs and price. Why is this so important? If you have a nice instrument, you'll want to play.

Take the time to really examine each instrument's neck and fretboard with your eyes and your hands. You'll notice some brands have wider fretboards, while others have thicker necks. These variables could be important to you. For example, in my search, I found that I prefer ukuleles with wider necks because they give my fingers a bit more room on the fretboard. Once I discovered this, it helped me narrow my search, as not all brands make ukes with a wider fretboard.

LOOKS AREN'T EVERYTHING

You may see a uke hanging on the wall that you think is ugly, or just doesn't seem special. However, once you play it, you might discover that its voice is amazing. Take a chance to play all the instruments that you can, even if you don't think that any of the available ukes will be the one. If possible, bring a friend (who plays) with you on this search. I like to narrow down the uke choices to my top three or five favorites, and then have someone play each for me while I close my eyes and listen. Once you take your eyes out of the equation, you're judging the uke on its sound, not by its looks. If I don't have a friend to help me, I may just pick up each instrument, close my eyes, and play so I can focus on the feel of the instrument and its sound.

Don't get hung up on the wood. Yes, koa is a beautiful wood and it's traditional, but that doesn't mean it's "the best" wood for ukuleles. I know this sounds blasphemous, but have an open mind. I'm always surprised by what sounds great—and here's the kicker—what I think sounds great might not be what you think sounds great.

II.
INSIDE THE STORE
BY MIM

CHECK THE SPECS FIRST

Manufacturers and retailers often label laminate ukuleles as simply the name of the wood. For example, a laminate mahogany ukulele will be labeled "mahogany," while a ukulele with solid wood will be labeled "solid mahogany." So look for the word "solid" if you are looking for a solid top or all-solid instrument. If in doubt, ask the retailer or look up the model online. I have known ukulele players who have assumed they owned a solid instrument when it was, in fact, a laminate.

CHECK THE TUNERS

Even if the ukulele is in tune, make sure you tune it down and then back up again to make sure the gears of the tuners are turning smoothly and not grinding. If the ukulele has friction tuners, and it is not staying in tune, ask the retailer to tighten the screw on the back of the tuner, so you can adequately tune and try out the ukulele.

CHECK THE NUT

Barre chords should not be hard to make. If you cannot make a B♭chord easily and you have no physical issues that inhibit your ability to make a barre chord, then you should easily be able to make a B♭ chord. Too many ukulele players think their inability to make the basic barre chords has to do with their skill level. I often ask them if they mind me checking out their ukulele, and most of the time the problem is that the nut is way too high. With a few simple adjustments, in less than

five minutes, they go from barre chord failure to success. Also, give the open strings a nice hard pluck. If any of the strings rattle at all, it may be that the nut of your ukulele is cut too low.

CHECK THE FRETS

This is very important and very easy to do. Check the frets by plucking every string on every fret of the ukulele and listening for a metallic or annoying buzzing sound. And don't be shy—really pluck every note on the fretboard. Unlevel frets are very common in ukuleles of all price points. When a string is fretted, the ukulele will rattle and buzz if there is a high fret higher up the fretboard. Often, players think a note that does not ring clear is due to their inexperience and improper finger placement, but high frets are very common and often overlooked as the cause of a buzzy ukulele.

CHECK THE SADDLE

The action is normally measured at the 12th fret. I do not like to give specific measurements for the action at the 12th fret, because each size, brand, and build of ukulele has different measurements they can

accommodate. So a good guideline is to make sure the ukulele is easy to play up the neck and that the strings do not feel overly high. If your saddle is high, it is often to compensate for high frets, so make sure your frets are level before you have the saddle taken down.

CHECK THE TONE

When a customer comes to my shop, the number of choices can often be overwhelming and they say to me, "How am I possibly going to choose?" My answer is that we are going to treat this like an eye exam for your ears. I play two ukes back-to-back, they eliminate one, and it goes back on the wall. Then I play the "winner" with another ukulele and they pick a favorite of those two, and so on, until it is down to one ukulele. Sometimes it's love-at-first-uke, and sometimes it takes time to narrow it down to the proper ukulele for the player. So my advice is to take your time, and play every uke. If you are a new player and are uncomfortable playing on your own, ask the retailer to play the ukuleles for you. Sometimes getting the audience perspective of a ukulele's tone will help you decide. 𝓊

SOUND ADVICE

5 overlooked features to consider
when buying your first (or next)
'really good' ukulele
BY DOUGLAS REYNOLDS

If "Ukulele Acquisition Syndrome" strikes and a higher-quality instrument is in your future, you want to get it right. Everyone's hands, ears, and tastes are unique. But beyond how an instrument feels, sounds, or calls to you, there are some often overlooked features to consider. These apply whether you're purchasing "off-the-rack" or having a custom ukulele built just for you. Here are five options to look for while shopping:

Lichty Long Neck Tenor's soundport

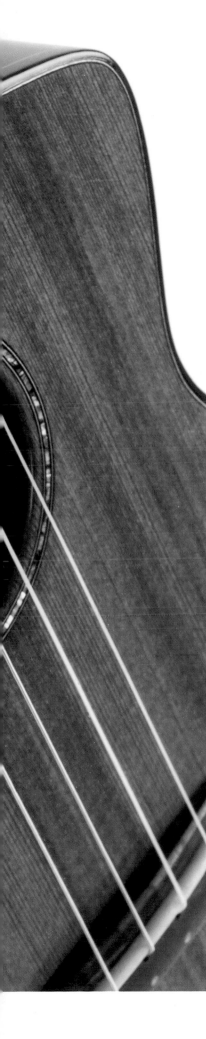

1. RADIUSED FRETBOARD

This feature is a must for me. Most ukuleles have flat fretboards. If you plan on playing a lot of barre chords, a slightly curved fretboard might just change your world. Not sure if you have a radiused fingerboard? One way to check is to rest your chin on your uke's strings over the sound hole and stare down the length of the fretboard. The wood and fret wires across the width of the neck will likely be completely flat. Most acoustic guitars have slightly curved or "radiused fretboards," and this feature is now finding favor with some ukulele builders. The term refers to the radius, in inches, of the circle that would be created if that slight curve were to be extended a complete 360 degrees. [Ed note: Shorter radiuses mean a more curved fingerboard.] Why does this slight curve make such a difference? Fingers naturally curve at rest. When barring your index finger across all four strings, your middle knuckle can press hard against the wood on a flat fretboard. Over time, this can cause discomfort and fatigue. Although the curve of a radiused fretboard is slight, it reduces strain and makes for a more comfortable playing experience.

2. ZERO-FRET

This is a case in which zero is more! A zero-fret is an extra fret placed just inside the nut. There are tonal advantages for using a zero-fret, such as making open strings sound more like fretted notes, but it also reduces the finger pressure needed to play at the first fret. Why? The nut is much taller than the fret wires, causing the strings at that position to sit higher. The string between the nut and first fret is also at its shortest. These two factors make it tough for newer players to handle the pesky B♭ chord, not to mention B♭m or C#7. A zero-fret reduces that negative combination by half. Your fingers will thank you. Zero-frets are not new, nor are they reserved solely for custom instruments. Unfortunately, "off the rack" ukuleles with zero-frets are somewhat rare, but they do exist. Certainly, if you are having a new ukulele built, ask for this terrific option.

3. WIDER NECK

Ukulele neck-width specifications are measured at the nut. Most ukuleles have a nut width of 1-3/8 inches, but some offer wider nuts, up to 1.5 inches. That extra 1/8-inch divided over four strings might not seem like much, but if you have large hands or thick fingers, a wider neck will make you feel like you just traded in your regular mattress for a king size!

4. EXTRA SIDE DOTS

Dots on the side of a ukulele's neck are extremely beneficial for newer players. They are easily installed on any ukulele and can help you track which frets you are playing on. I recommend dots at the third, fifth, seventh, tenth, and 12th frets. Most ukes have dots on the front of the fretboard, but don't be seduced into using them for neck navigation—they can actually make playing more difficult! Eye-catching decorations on the face of your fretboard can coerce you into tilting the uke back toward you. This over-extends the curve of your fretting hand's wrist and puts a strain on all the components that make up this remarkably complex joint. Even after playing for many years, my custom ukuleles have blank fretboards for this very reason. To give your fretting hand the most strength, your ukulele should be held perpendicular to the floor or even tilted slightly away from you. Resist the urge to peek over the neck. Embrace your side dots!

5. SOUNDPORT

This somewhat recent option in ukulele-building is a hole on the side of the ukulele, instead of the front, that directs a little more volume and tone toward your ears. You're playing music! Why not hear it as clearly as possible? *u*

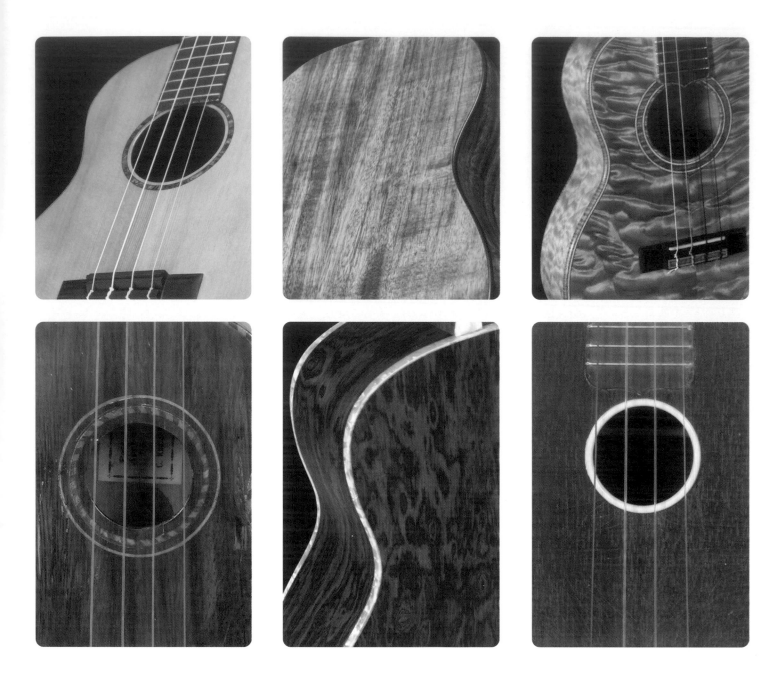

INSIDE THE WOOD SHOP

A luthier explains the 'whys' and 'hows' of ukulele tonewoods

BY DAVE SIGMAN

It all starts with the wood. From the entry-level, factory-made ukuleles produced overseas to the high-end custom instruments fashioned by skilled luthiers, selecting the right wood for the job is where it all begins. The two main criteria in wood selection are, of course, beauty and, perhaps more important, tonal quality. As a custom ukulele builder, a big part of my job is selecting the woods I'm going to use. When shopping for a ukulele, it's good to be informed about the wood, why it was selected, and how it affects the sound.

SOUNDBOARD WOOD

Where sound is concerned, probably the most important wood in the whole instrument is the top (also known as the soundboard) and the wood used in the soundboard bracing (the reinforcing pieces glued to the top inside the instrument). Commonly used woods for a uke's soundboard include koa, mahogany, cedar, and various types of spruce.

When selecting a suitable soundboard, I first do a visual inspection of the wood to make sure the piece has a nice, even grain and no flaws. I then gently flex the board, checking it for stiffness across the grain. Stiffer is better. If the potential soundboard is too flexible, the sound quality can be compromised—resulting in less volume, a lack of sustain, or tonal imbalance. Finally, I check the "tap tone," holding the board up between my thumb and index finger and tapping it to produce what will hopefully be a nice, clear tone.

Many species of wood improve tonally with age, most notably Sitka spruce. I've noticed that right after stringing up a new uke for the first time, the sound may be a bit quieter for a while, but this will soon change. The low notes become deeper, the high notes brighter, and the sustain longer, all in the first hour of life. The sound quality will continue to open up and mature for several months.

I've seen beautiful ukes built with dazzling woods that are a delight to behold, but lacking in tonal quality due to mediocre wood selection of the soundboard and supportive bracing. Think of how a stereo speaker works. It's a box made of wood back and sides with a lightweight paper cone in front that vibrates and pushes out the sound waves. A ukulele body works in much the same way. The more freely the top is able to vibrate, the more efficiently sound waves will be produced.

Córdoba's 35TS tenor uke is built with acacia back and sides, and solid Sitka spruce for its top.

This tenor uke by luthier Steve Grimes has a body that's completely made out of quilted maple.

A lot of entry-level, factory-made ukuleles are constructed with laminated wood, which is created by bonding together thin layers of inexpensive, wood with an outer layer of an exotic or decorative veneer. This method of production is less expensive than solid-wood construction. I've played quite a few ukes made with laminates and found the majority of them to have pretty decent sound, though they're generally not as dynamic as a higher-end instrument.

However, they do offer some advantages. The lower price tag makes the uke more affordable, of course, and a good choice for a first uke. The laminate construction, while making the uke a bit heavier, also makes it sturdy, so a laminate-wood uke is a good choice for kids. They also make great travel ukes—the laminate construction may stand up better to the varying changes in climate one may encounter during travels.

BACK & SIDES WOODS

Probably the most common wood choice for the back and sides of ukuleles is Hawaiian koa. Koa works beautifully as a top as well, producing a warm, mellow tone that really evokes the island feeling. That, along with its exotic color and grain, makes it the tonewood of choice for many.

Honduras mahogany is also widely used in uke construction. It is quite similar to koa in density, workability, and sound quality and, like koa, it's also used in ukes where a single kind of wood is used for the entire body— the soundboard as well as the back and sides of the instrument.

One of my favorite wood choices for ukes that use the same wood for the entire body is claro walnut, a California native that is similar to koa and mahogany in terms of stability and tonal character. And, like koa, choice pieces of claro walnut exhibit very curly, dramatic grain. Many other species of wood, both imported and domestic, are used in uke body construction as well, including maple, sycamore, madrone, myrtle, ebony, monkey pod, a wide variety of rosewoods, and even bamboo laminates. In recent years there has been a move among some makers to even more exotic but sustainable woods, such as bocote, quilted ash, mango, ziricote, camphor burl, macawood, zebrawood—it seems like almost anything goes!

Rosewood is also widely used and much prized for its beauty and distinctive bright sound. There are several varieties well-suited to uke construction: East Indian rosewood, Honduras rosewood, and cocobolo to name a few. These are all true rosewoods, of the Dalbergia family. Brazilian rosewood once considered the "holy grail" of all tonewoods, is now subject to several trade restrictions, which means that it has become expensive and difficult to find in good quality.

NECK WOOD

The most commonly used wood for the necks of ukuleles is probably Honduras mahogany. It has nice, even grain and it is stable and easy to work with. It also has an impressive strength-to-weight ratio, making for a well-balanced instrument that feels right in the player's hands.

Many other woods work well for necks, too. I often use koa, if it's not too dense. Spanish cedar also works well and is the traditional choice for flamenco guitar necks. Sometimes I'll get a client who requests a neck made with wood that is similar to the wood used in the body, so I may go with black walnut on a darker uke or maple on a lighter one.

FINGERBOARD AND BRIDGE

There are several wood choices available for the fingerboard, but I generally choose a hardwood like ebony or rosewood. The fingerboard takes a lot of wear and must be tough enough to stand up to the abrasion of the strings as well as the player's fingers. I once saw a very old Hawaiian uke with a koa fingerboard that had holes between the frets all the way through the fingerboard and into the neck wood! This uke had clearly been to quite a few luaus. Koa is commonly used for fingerboard and bridges, too. However, it's best to pick a dense piece. Hardwoods are also better suited to hold the tang of the fret wire, as well as any decorative inlays, firmly in place on the fingerboard.

The bridge, like the fingerboard, should be a select piece of hardwood, completely dried and free of any defects. I usually match the fingerboard and bridge woods for aesthetic purposes. The tension of the strings on the bridge is considerable—about 35 pounds is exerted on a low-G tenor uke. That's a lot of weight, but not as much as on a steel-string guitar, where the pull is closer to 160 pounds.

EDGE BINDING

In selecting the binding for the edges of the body, I usually pick a hardwood that creates a nice contrast and compliments the body wood. For example, if the uke body is a straight-grained, darker wood, like rosewood, I might pick a lighter, curly wood, like koa or maple. Conversely, on an instrument with highly figured grain, I would choose an edge binding that's less showy. Basically, if it's a plain wood, I use fancy binding, and for a more figured wood, plain binding.

The binding's job, besides looking nice, is to protect the edge of the uke from bumps and bruises and to help hold the body together. That being said, there are a lot of ukes out there with no edge binding at all. Some builders use a decorative "rope" binding, a series of alternating light and dark wood edging around the body, giving the instrument a vintage look. Plastic bindings are commonly used, too, and are available in different colors and patterns, such as ivoroid, pearloid, and faux tortoiseshell.

WOOD & ITS IMPACT ON TONE

So how do you know what kind of wood your uke should be made of? It depends to some extent on what kind of sound you prefer.

If you mostly play solo, a warm, well-rounded tone, like that produced by an all-koa uke or one with a mahogany or cedar top, might suit you. Or maybe you play in a group and you need your solo licks to soar above the guitars. Then perhaps a uke with a rosewood body and a spruce top will deliver the bright, punchy sound you're after. The list of possible combinations is as vast as the number of wood species.

Just remember: The most aesthetically pleasing woods are not necessarily the best sounding, so take time to audition as many ukes as possible to help inform your purchasing decision. *u*

Kala's KA-BC-CT concert uke uses bocote wood for its back and sides.

This vintage Lyon & Healy Bell uke has a body made out of mahogany.

Koa has long been a popular choice for ukes of all types, as evidenced by this vintage Knutsen harp ukulele.

PLUGGED IN, READY TO GO

Quick tips for performance gear

BY CRAIG CHEE

Part of being a seasoned performer is understanding every aspect of your performance. This includes everything that helps carry your sound to the ears of your audience. Here is a quick rundown of pickups and effects that can affect your sound.

PICKUPS

PASSIVE PICKUPS
(K&K, Fishman AG Series, etc.)
Pros: Wider dynamic range and supposedly more "natural"-sounding; no battery means that the ukulele is lighter.

Cons: Prone to feedback, especially when there are other instruments onstage; requires a pre-amp (such as an L.R. Baggs Venue DI or Fishman Aura Spectrum DI) to boost the signal to the soundboard.

ACTIVE PICKUPS
(L.R. Baggs 5.0, Fishman Pro-Blend, etc.)
Pros: Battery-powered onboard preamp produces a cleaner sound with much less "body" noise compared to a passive pickup; easier to shape your sound with the onboard EQ.

Cons: Heavier due to the battery; more things can go wrong since the pickup system is a bit more complicated.

PEDALS

COMPRESSOR A compressor pedal helps on two fronts. Because a ukulele performance can be very dynamic (such as going from strumming to fingerpicking), a compressor can help make our sound a bit more consistent by smoothing out some of those harder hits. The other way that a compressor can be used is to help boost our ukulele's sustain. These tiny instruments don't have as much natural sustain as a guitar, so a pedal like the Boss CS-3 Compression Sustainer is a fantastic tool to help cleanly increase your sustain and to give more options and feel to your playing.

REVERB Because of its small size and somewhat limited note range, the ukulele is not the fullest-sounding instrument out there. Since it emulates the effect of sound bouncing off walls, a reverb pedal will instantly give more body to your ukulele's sound. Reverb can also be used to help create an effect that would be impossible to achieve in a space, such as making a small room sound like a cathedral. I always warn my students to tread lightly with this effect because too much can be a distraction to your sound. One of my favorite reverb pedals is the TC Electronic Hall of Fame, but as with all these categories of gear, there are many to choose from.

LOOPER A looper can be an incredible tool both on and off the stage. Ukulele artists like Kalei Gamiao and Karlie Goya often create a whole backing band by utilizing different "layers" of sounds. Loopers can also be very helpful as a practice tool for working on your timing and improvising. You can record yourself playing the chords in a section of a song and then practice soloing over your chords. Many of us did this the old-fashioned way—by recording ourselves playing a progression over and over on an old cassette recorder and then playing it back while practicing the solo or other phrases along with it. *u*

Mim and some strings in her Virginia shop.

THINGS ABOUT STRINGS

What you need to know about this vital part of your ukulele
BY MIM

F or your ukulele to make music you need strings! Sounds easy, right? Well, if you go on the internet and simply ask, "Which ukulele strings are the best?" you will get hundreds of opinions. Why? Because at the end of the day, it really comes down to personal preference. Think of it this way: If you gather a group of people together and ask them their favorite color, you are bound to get a variety of responses. The same holds true with ukulele players and strings. If you gather a group of ukulele players together and ask them about their favorite strings, you are in for a lot more information than you bargained for.

When I am asked which ukulele string is best, my answer is, "Whatever strings you like!" If you catch me on a good day, you may get a few recommendations out of me. Giving a solid string recommendation is hard because my ears, my fingertips, and my playing style are bound to be different than yours. So in this article, I will do my best to provide guidance on string selection without endorsing one type of string over another. This way you can make an informed decision that is best for you.

WHEN CHOOSING UKULELE STRINGS, KEEP THESE THREE THINGS IN MIND:

1. STRINGS ARE CHEAP

Most strings do not cost a lot of money. It never hurts to grab a few different packs of strings, and when it is time for a string change, throw a new set on and give them a try.

2. STRINGS ARE TEMPORARY

They are meant to be changed. If you love them, great! If you don't, on to the next set. Just keep a set of your go-to strings on hand to switch back to.

3. STRINGS ARE SUBJECTIVE

A string that sounds and feels great to you, may not to someone else—and that is OK.

With these three things in mind, strings can be a fun and affordable way to conduct your own tone experiments on your ukulele. You may also be surprised to find that a string you love on one ukulele may not bring out the best in another. When you take into account the size, wood, and build of your ukulele, then mix in your own preferences for tone and feel, there really is no way to give any string the sought-after label of "best ukulele string."

It is important to keep in mind that it can take strings anywhere from hours to days to settle into their tone. They need to stretch into place. So instead of giving up on them immediately, give them a few days to a week to settle in before you declare them rubbish.

THINGS TO CONSIDER WHEN CHOOSING A STRING SET:

MATERIAL

It is impossible to cover every string material in a general essay like this. Companies are always innovating to add unique and interesting strings into the ukulele market. So, although this is not an all-inclusive list, most strings can be lumped into the following subcategories:

SYNTHETIC GUT

Ukulele strings were originally made out of gut, which is exactly what it sounds like: the intestinal lining of sheep or goats, usually, and sometimes cattle. You can still buy them, but they are rare and expensive. There are many companies that have made great strides in replicating the density, tone, and feel of gut strings with synthetic materials. These strings tend to be warm, with a punchy mid-range tone, and tend to have great longevity. There is a wide variety of affordable synthetic options.

"

What works on my instrument may sound terrible on yours. The joy of ukulele is that strings are inexpensive, and you can try many. I'll generally order seven or so sets when I get a new instrument and give them all a go to see what suits it best. The instrument will always tell you what it does and doesn't like"

—CHRISTOPHER DAVIS-SHANNON

NYLON

Made from a variety of nylon polymers, the exact feel and tone of nylon strings can vary from brand to brand. Smooth and easy to play, nylon strings give an ukulele a more mellow tone, with a distinct punch and warmth. One common complaint about nylon strings is that they are very "stretchy," so they require a lot more tuning. So be sure to allocate a few extra days for them to settle in if you choose to try nylon strings.

FLUOROCARBON

Most fluorocarbon strings produce a bright, crisp, resonant tone, which I often describe as "smooth." These strings are generally smooth to the touch, too, and often easy on the fingertips. But again, there are so many varieties, each set can produce a different feel and sound depending on gauge and tension. Fishing line is also made of fluorocarbon and comes in a variety of gauges, so many players have been known to experiment with different string gauges via their local sporting goods store, to see what combination they like best on their ukulele. Fluorocarbon strings are also known for their longevity and and holding their tune well. They tend to be far less stretchy and settle into their tuning more quickly.

WOUND STRINGS

These are generally nylon strings that are wrapped in a metal or polymer material to create lower tones without adding a lot of density to the lower-voiced strings. They are often found in low-G, tenor, or baritone sets. They have their own unique booming low voice. Their main drawback is they often do not last as long as the other strings, often wearing out, corroding, or unraveling before the other strings in the set. Luckily, many can be purchased individually so you can replace just that one string. They also tend to squeak more than regular nylon or fluorocarbon strings.

GAUGE

The gauge is the thickness, or diameter, of a specific string. Why is this important to note? If the nut, where your string rests, is cut for a thinner string, a thicker-gauge string may sit too high, making the string action high and therefore making your instrument difficult to play. Conversely, if a nut has been cut for a thicker gauge string, a smaller gauge string may sit too low, causing a buzz when you open strum. Both of these issues can be fixed in a matter of minutes by an experienced ukulele tech. My advice is, if you have a solid string preference, you may want to have your ukulele set up to accommodate that specific string.

Your playing style may also lend itself to thicker or thinner strings. A thicker gauge often has a louder, harder-hitting, bold voice that is a favorite among more aggressive strummers. The smaller gauges are often favored by those who are looking for a crisp, light, intricate sound.

TENSION

String tension is how many pounds of pressure a string exerts when at pitch. So, in the simplest terms, tension is how tight a string feels. The higher the tension, the tighter the string. Higher-tension strings can give a bigger, bolder, more aggressive sound, but can also be harder to fret. A lot of players with an aggressive playing style tend to favor higher tension. The lower-tension strings are easier to fret but have a looser feel. They often have a warmer and richer tone. They are what I recommend for children and people with hand-strength issues, or arthritis. A low-tension string paired with a low setup can be a game changer for a new player or someone with finger pain!

LOW-G VS. HIGH-G

The ukulele is traditionally tuned G C E A, with the G string being a high G, and the tuning dropping down for the C, and then going up to the E and then to the A. This is called reentrant tuning. It gives your playing that distinct, traditional, bright and lively ukulele sound. Most ukuleles come with a high-G string. Low-G, also known as linear tuning, is when the G string is tuned an octave lower than the traditional tuning, lower than the C string. This expands the range of notes that can be achieved on the ukulele by five. The ukulele then has a more warm, rich, and low tone to it, more similar to a guitar.

Which one is right for you? Again, it depends on your preferences and playing style. Some musicians have more than one ukulele, one strung low-G and one strung high-G, for different songs. Some just stick to one tuning. If you don't know which is right

for you, my advice is to buy a single wound low-G string. Thanks to the material they're wrapped with, wound G strings provide the lower tone without drastically affecting the diameter of the string. Therefore, most wound low-G strings fit nicely in nut slots that have been cut for a high-G string. You can replace just the G string and see if you like the sound, and then you can always go back to the high-G if it is not for you.

When choosing a low-G set, keep in mind that most string sets achieve the lower octave pitch by either offering a wound string or increasing the gauge of the string. If you choose a set with a larger-gauge low-G string, you may need a slight adjustment so that the string does not sit too high in the nut slot.

WHEN TO CHANGE STRINGS

There is no solid time frame for when you should change your strings. A lot depends on how often you play, how aggressively you play, and whether you exclusively play one ukulele or spread out your playing among different ukes. Usually, the first sign that your strings need to be changed is when your ukulele starts to sound a little "off." It might seem a little dull, not hold its tune, and the intonation won't sound quite right. Intonation is how well your string stays in tune as you play up the fretboard. Whenever someone expresses concern that their intonation is off, I ask them when they last changed their strings. Most seem to be skeptical that the answer is so simple, but after they change their strings and allow them to settle for a few days, the intonation issues are usually resolved. Strings are in a constant state of being stretched, and therefore a time will come when they are literally stretched too thin, and the intonation will be sharp.

The other obvious time to change your strings is if they are damaged, show a lot of wear, or if you want to just try a new string set for fun!

OTHER THINGS TO CONSIDER

This is where I will dispense some insight that does not fit neatly into categories, but I think is important to note when it comes to strings. Strings are not a "magic pill" that will make you play better. They are a tool for your musicianship. Though they may not improve your playing, the right strings can make you want to practice more if they are easy to play, appeal to your ear, and bring out the best in your ukulele. But needless to say, strings cannot replace practice!

Keep in mind, you most likely won't find a one-string-fits-all solution. Depending on the size, tonewood, brand, and build of your ukulele, you may find you prefer one type of string on one ukulele and another type on a different ukulele. I have one set I love on my spruce concert, but it does not bring out the best on my mahogany soprano. I also have a set I like for my upbeat and lively songs, and another I like when I want to bring out the dark warmth of my koa ukulele.

What if you don't want to spend money, time, and hassle of trial and error? If you are lucky enough to have an ukulele community in your area, you can attend a jam or festival and ask to try out ukuleles that are strung differently than yours. If you like the way the strings sound and feel, ask what they are and try them out on

your own ukulele. If you are unable to meet with other players, you can find a lot of great demos online, so you can at least hear how they sound.

Sometimes, it is not your strings. The proper strings can certainly bring out the best in your ukulele. If your ukulele is built in such a way that it has a slightly dull tone, you may note some improvement when you change the strings, but the ukulele itself may not be able to achieve the tone you are looking for. A string set is an easy way to troubleshoot any tone issues.

Some strings are easier to fret, but if your ukulele has high action (the string height above the fretboard), or structural issues, even the lightest gauge strings may be hard to fret. When this happens, my advice would be to see a skilled technician about getting your ukulele set up properly. A great setup can be the difference between you loving your ukulele or giving up in frustration. I set up thou-

sands of ukuleles a year and am a firm believer in the power of a great setup!

Learn to change your own strings. It is not as hard as it seems. I have had many people say they never change their own strings. Often they are afraid of damaging their instrument, but in fact It is very hard to damage your ukulele while changing the strings. I have been changing strings for ten years and have yet to damage an ukulele during a string change. (See the next page for easy to follow tips on changing strings.) Your first few tries will be awkward and take you forever, but before you know it you'll be helping your friends learn to change their strings!

In closing, don't overthink it. Have fun! Strings are strings. They are a fun way to tweak the tone of your ukulele. Don't worry too much about finding the Holy Grail of strings; use the ones that feel good and bring you joy when you play! *u*

CHANGE YOUR UKE STRINGS IN 7 EASY STEPS

BY GREG OLWELL

JOEY LUSTERMAN PHOTOS

Changing strings is something every ukulele player will need to do at some point. Uke strings don't break often and can last a long time, so you might not need to change your strings as often as guitarists or other stringed-instrument players. But it might happen someday, and when it does, you should know how to do it right.

The first question is: When do you need to do it? Because today's strings are so durable, you'll rarely be forced to change them. Still, over time your strings will become worn and eventually sound a little dead.

More than just replacing worn-out or broken strings, changing your strings is also the quickest and cheapest way to enhance the sound of your ukulele. Even using the same set from the same manufacturer can make a surprising difference. A fresh set of strings can sound so much zippier and livelier; it can breathe new life into your instrument.

When putting on strings, I like to start on one side and work my way across. (It doesn't matter which direction you go, but I usually begin with the bottom strings—the G string on most ukuleles—and work my way to the higher strings, repeating the following steps for each string.) Some ukuleles, like my main concert uke, have a slotted bridge, which allows me to simply tie a knot on one end and slide the string into the slot. However, since most ukuleles have a bridge that's similar to that of a classical guitar, these steps focus on that style of bridge.

There are plenty of ways to change strings, but I've found this method works well on every instrument, holds the strings securely, and helps you get in tune quickly.

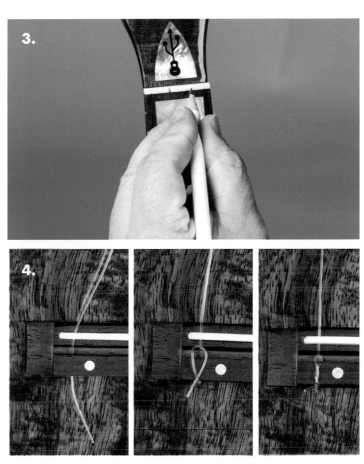

1. START BY GATHERING THE THINGS YOU'LL NEED

Make sure to have your ukulele, a cloth, a tuner, a pencil, and a wire cutter (or, if you're in a pinch, scissors) handy. It's easy to accidentally grab the wrong-size set of strings at the store, so make sure you have the right strings for your uke before you begin.

2. HOUSE CLEANING

I like to do a little cleaning once I've removed the strings. Having the strings off makes it easier to reach those places under the strings that attract dust, like near the bridge or around the tuners. If your fingerboard has accumulated some gunk, you can clean it off by gently rubbing your fingerboard along the wood grain with extra-fine steel wool (0000 grade) to remove the buildup without harming the wood. Bonus: It also shines up the frets.

3. SMOOTH RUNNING

Use a sharpened pencil to add a little graphite ("pencil lead") to each slot on your ukulele's nut. This helps the strings slide smoothly through the slots.

4. TIE-UP

Now you can anchor the string to the bridge. Start by feeding one end of the string through the back of the bridge, then wrap it around itself. Get it snug around the base of the bridge, then wrap the excess under the string once, then twice. This keeps the string from slipping. Pull it tightly into place so the string is now anchored.

5. PEGHEAD END

I like to wind the string around the peg three times—more than that might cause the peg to get messy and can interfere with tuning, while fewer turns might be a little less secure. To do this, I mark the point by crimping the string about 1-1/2 to 2 inches past the peg. Feed the string through the hole until the crimp is through the peg hole.

6. WIND 'EM UP

Now it's time to start winding the string. A string winder can help speed up the process, but the method is the same with or without one. Wrap the first turn above the tuning peg's hole, then just before you complete one full turn, push it down below the hole and continue winding. This wraps the string around the excess length and holds the string tightly so that it doesn't slip. Continue winding until you bring the string up to pitch.

7. FINISHING UP

You should have three or four neatly wound turns of string on the peg. Use your wire cutter to snip off the excess string. Repeat for each string.   *u*

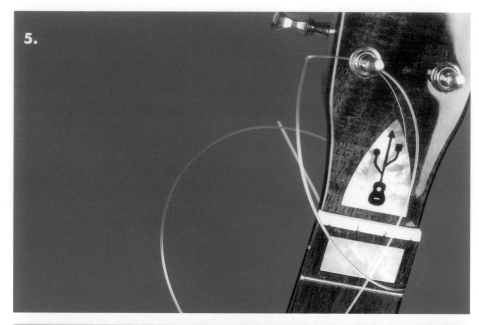

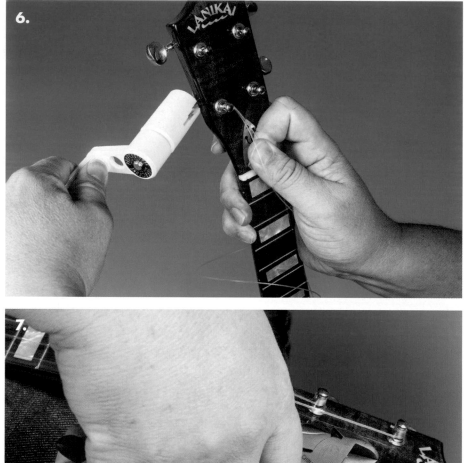

WHY WON'T MY UKE STAY IN TUNE?

Four tips that may make a difference in your sound

BY MAMIE MINCH

We all know there's just something great about ukuleles. You can use them as a simple way to work out chords to a tune or accompany yourself while singing a melody. They're a great excuse to make friends and connect with people—I hear George Harrison always traveled with two! When they behave, they're trusty little friends who are always ready to have a good time. But often, ukuleles have tuning issues that are particular to them. Some of them happen right off the bat, while others appear as a beloved instrument starts to fall into the "vintage" category. Let's start with the simplest possible answer for players wondering why their ukulele won't stay in tune.   >>

Lift the string out of the nut and stretch it like this to help it stabilize.

2. CHECK FOR WORN-OUT TUNERS

Friction tuners, often seen on vintage ukes, are the simplest form of tuning machine, but they can be tricky. It's not unusual for the cardboard washer inside the tuner to flatten and stop gripping, making the tuner fail to hold tune. You can tell that is happening if the screw at the end of the button is tight (don't over-tighten it!) and the entire thing still spins. In this case, a good repair shop with vintage experience can help you, either to replace the tuners—not an expensive item—or possibly to fix your vintage ones if you really love how they look.

If they are newer, geared tuners, there's a chance they were installed poorly. One way to check is to tug on a string: Does the tuner shaft pull forward? It's possible that one of the screws holding the plate to the headstock is loose. Make sure the screws are snug, using the right size screwdriver to avoid stripping out the screw's head.

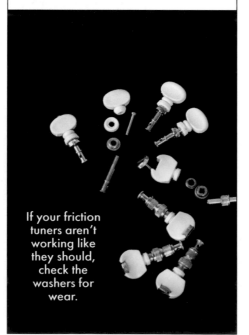

If your friction tuners aren't working like they should, check the washers for wear.

1. STRETCH YOUR STRINGS

Most modern ukulele strings are made from some version of nylon—which is stretchy! It's not enough to just put your new strings on and tune up your instrument; you'll notice the strings go flat right away. Here's what to do: Once your strings are on and tuned up, grab one string at a time and pull it gently up and away from the fingerboard. The string will go flat, and you'll tune it back up to pitch. Repeat until stretching no longer makes your string go flat. This will improve the stability of your tuning. Also, be sure to tune *up* to pitch, not down, as this will ensure that your string doesn't slip a bit on the tuner shaft and go flat.

3. ARE YOU STRUMMING HARD ALL THE TIME?

Walloping on your strings can be a ton of fun. But if you hit your uke really hard for a while, you'll begin to notice that the strings won't hold pitch. It's no surprise when you think about the springiness of nylon ukulele strings; each time you strum, the strings stretch just a little. If you find that your already-stretched strings have a hard time behaving after you rock out particularly hard, that's why.

A non-compensated saddle (left) may not intonate as well as a compensated saddle (right).

4. INHERENT INTONATION ISSUES

So, now that we've talked about all the things we can do to help our instruments get in tune and stay in tune, it's time to talk about something that's functionally beyond our control: intonation!

The four strings on a ukulele—on all ukes, from soprano to baritone—are each of quite different thicknesses. This means that the strings need to have slightly different lengths to be able to play in tune along the fingerboard. Generally, the thinnest string is pulled forward to be the shortest, and the fattest string is pulled back to be the longest. (An electric guitar will have six adjustable saddles to slightly lengthen or shorten each string's scale length to help intonate it. In this way, the diameter of the strings is compensated for; a fatter string needs a little more length to intonate than its thinner neighbor.) Ukuleles generally have a straight saddle, with very little room to compensate for different string thicknesses. For this reason, while you may get one, or some, of your strings to intonate well up the neck, you probably won't get all of them to play in tune.

As if that's not enough, inexpensive ukuleles are often built with less quality control than we wish. I figure it's to help the manufacturer save time, and therefore deliver you a product at a lower price. Unfortunately, sometimes *none* of the strings intonate in tune.

A common and really frustrating problem is that many ukuleles are built with the bridge glued in the wrong place! Can this be fixed? Your tech could do a couple of things to massage the scale length to help your ukulele play more in tune, such as cant the saddle takeoff point back, or occasionally fill and reroute a saddle slot. But to really get to the bottom of the issue, she would need to re-glue the bridge in the right spot—and even then, getting all of the strings to intonate would be a tough job. In any case, this will often fall into the category of an inadvisable repair, as the repair bill would very likely be more expensive than the instrument itself.

It's like a perfect little life lesson wrapped up in the cute guise of your favorite four-stringed instrument. Rarely does life go exactly as we wish. So, relax! Sing a little Cliff Edwards! At least you have a ukulele to keep you company. *u*

PROTECT AND PRESERVE

Bags, cases & accessories for ukuleles

BY GREG OLWELL

While it doesn't take much more than a ukulele and a few chords to have tremendous fun, there are many accessories that might make your playing more comfortable, in tune, and expressive. Many of these accessories also give you a chance to show off your individuality, creativity, and to show that you're serious about having fun. Plus, it's probably safe to say that a few of us like shopping, and once you start looking at accessories, you'll find that there are uncountable numbers of tuners and gig bags to choose from, to name just two categories. To organize the broad mishmash of things that can be considered accessories, let's break them into a few subcategories by function: protection, instrument care and display, and accessories that may help you play better.

The Kanile'a 2020 Platinum Limited in its cushy case.

PROTECTION

Gig bags and cases are the first line of defense for your ukulele and can protect your four-string friend from dings and bumps. And perhaps more important, even the most basic cloth bag acts like a little enclosed shelter to keep your uke more stable and safe from changes in temperature and humidity. New materials and innovations keep blurring the differences between gig bags and cases, but generally, a case has a protective outer shell and an inner padded compartment to cradle your uke snugly, while a gig bag is lighter and softer, offering light-to-medium protection.

Most makers offer cases and gig bags to fit the instruments they sell, but since some of those OEM (original equipment manufacturer) bags and cases aren't snappy enough for natty ukulele players, the door is wide open for the booming business of sharp cases and bags. With designs ranging from tiki-inspired bamboo or floral patterns to plain black covers, cases and bags are a great way to stand out from the crowd and chances are you'll see a mind-blowing array of creativity and whimsy on parade wherever ukulele players gather.

Gig bags are perfect when maximum protection is not needed, which is most circumstances, and bags almost always have a strap or straps for carrying your uke on your shoulder, giving your hands some freedom. Another benefit of gig bags is that they often have more storage than hard cases do, giving you somewhere to put your other accessories. Some gig bags are not much more than a sack with a drawstring that you tuck your uke into after leaving a strum-along, while others may have substantial padding and be suitable for serious travel.

If protection is of serious importance to you, then consider a case. A case's primary benefit is a sturdy structure and they come in a couple of forms—hardshell and softshell. Hardshell cases have structures made out of plywood or lighter materials like ABS or even carbon fiber, and softshell cases often have the plush interior and molded padding of a hardshell case, with a lightweight woven exterior, usually made from nylon. Cases trade-off rugged protection for weight, and even with backpack straps, they're bulkier and heavier to carry around than a gig bag—but they can really save you in a pinch.

Many case makers offer gig bags in addition to hardshell and softshell cases, so when shopping make sure to check out the entire line to see if something catches your eye. Fremont offers vintage-styled tweed cases (starting at $90) and dazzling rugged gig bags; Guardian is one of the largest makers and has many bags and cases to choose from across a wide price range; Crossrock has molded ABS cases in vibrant colors ($76.99) and heavy-duty, thickly padded fiberglass shell cases ($198); and TKL is a big maker of original equipment cases and bags and they have bags starting at $55. The Fusion Urban ($140) is a feature-packed gig bag that I've seen several pros using on tour, but you don't have to spend more than $20 on a basic gig bag that will serve most players' needs for protection and portability. (All prices listed are as of 2020.)

One final piece of advice: Before you settle on a case or bag, take a moment to find out if the interior measurements of the case or bag you're shopping for fits your uke's dimensions. There is a lot of variety in ukulele shapes, even among ukes that are the same size, and one concert or tenor uke might be different from another, so measure your uke across the full length, the lower bout, and the depth, to make sure it fits in the case of your choice.

INSTRUMENT CARE & DISPLAY

Ukuleles are cute, beautiful instruments, and though the instrument may be humble, the people who play it can hardly be blamed for wanting to show off a little. To keep your ukulele in its best playable condition does not take much effort, but a few things can help you keep it playing its best and looking its best.

HUMIDIFIERS

As the weather changes during the course of a year, the relative humidity (RH) in our homes can rise or fall drastically and this can spell trouble for ukuleles made from wood. Wood is highly reactive to humidity and temperature changes, and a situation where the air gets too dry can lead to cracks, while too much moisture can loosen glue joints or make the body swell and sound muffled. Solid wood ukuleles are more affected by RH than laminated ones and for this reason it can be important to have a humidifier to keep your ukulele close to the ideal range of 40- to 60-percent relative humidity. The most powerful protection during dry times is to keep your instrument in its case with a humidifier. This small, controlled environment helps the humidifier act effectively. A few fit into your uke's soundhole, like the Music Nomad Humilele ($9.99), D'Addario Ukulele Humidifier Pro ($10.99), and Kyser Lifeguard ($19.95), while Oasis's trusted OH-18 ($19.95) is like a small water bottle that stays in the case. You might also consider getting a digital hygrometer, which can be found at any hardware or home supply store, to monitor the humidity in your home.

STANDS AND HOOKS

You're much more likely to pick up your ukulele and strum if it's easy to grab, and a stand or wall hook is a great way to keep your uke handy and safe, while also adding to your home decor. Some stands are foldable, so they're easy to tote to a club meeting, but many of the small floor stands are better suited for home. There are many to choose from, including the handsome, X-shaped Ohana US-20 stand ($25), while Cooperstand offers compact folding stands in wood ($49.95) or recycled ABS ($24.95). The Hercules Ukulele floor stand ($34.99) is a rugged tripod stand that is tall and suitable for the stage. If hanging them on the wall is more appealing, check out the String Swing Wall-Mount Ukulele Hanger ($12.99).

CLEANING

Old worn-out t-shirts work in a pinch to wipe smudges and dust off of your uke, but modern microfiber cloths do a much better job of keeping your uke clean. Rather than reusing a home cleaning cloth, consider getting a dedicated microfiber for cleaning your ukes—maybe from your favorite local shop or your uke maker. It won't get dirtied through other household uses and will be ready for you when you need it. Many modern finishes won't need to be polished and if you regularly give your uke a wipe-down, you may never need to apply polish, but some ukes may benefit from an occasional light polishing with some specialized compounds that are designed to work on instrument finishes, unlike some household products that might work well on the dining room table, but aren't suitable for instruments.

PERFORMANCE

When it comes to performing, there are a few items that can really improve the playing experience. Some might help you play better, while others might kick open doors for creativity and improvisation.

CLIP-ON TUNERS

At any ukulele get-together you'll see little clip-on tuners sprouting from the headstocks of many, if not most, ukuleles. Small, affordable, and often colorful, clip-on tuners can help you keep your uke from sounding sour, and that's reason enough for them to be an essential item for nearly every player. One benefit clip-ons have over smartphone tuning apps is that the tuner gets a clearer sense of the pitch, making it easier to tune in a noisy environment. Because they're so immensely useful and popular, there's a seemingly endless variety of them available, with two of the most popular chromatic tuners being the Snark SN-6X ($11.25) and D'Addario NS Micro headstock tuner ($20.39/two-pack). If you're interested taking in a more simple route, some tuners, like the low-profile Korg MiniPitch ($19.99), only display the four standard open string notes. Just remember to take off your tuner before you perform, for a more polished look onstage.

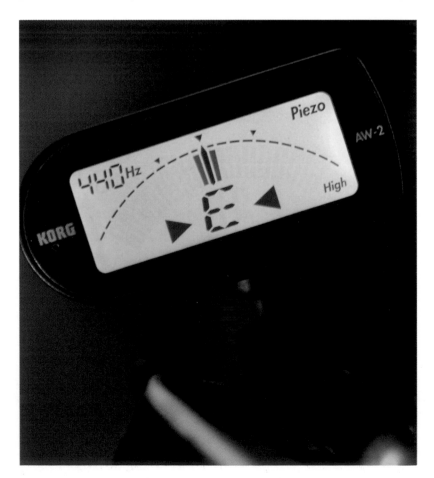

STRAPS

After the tuner and case, a strap might be the most popular ukulele accessory. Straps can free both arms up for making music and are almost essential for those players who have trouble holding the uke and playing, especially on the larger tenor and baritone sizes. Straps are available in a limitless variety of patterns, from basic black to fanciful aloha prints, and are a great way to show off a little personal style to go along with function. Just about anyone with a sewing machine can make one, so there are many options for buying from a one-person shop, and of course speciality strap makers, like Sherrin's Threads and Levy's have dozens (hundreds!) of styles to choose from. Many ukes will require the installation of a strap button or two and that's something that is easy to do if you have a drill, or a repair shop could handle it in seconds. Or, if you do not want to add strap buttons to your uke, there are non-invasive straps that hook to the bottom of the soundhole and support the uke from underneath, or others that wrap around the uke's body, like the Hug Strap. The only trouble a strap might give you is choosing a favorite pattern.

CAPOS

Many of us play the ukulele to accompany ourselves while we sing, but when a song's chord progression and melody don't suit our natural singing voices, a capo is an easy and effective way to change the key to be more suitable for your voice. Capos are small, removable devices that clamp to the fingerboard, slightly behind a fret, and change the tuning of your open strings. One of the neat things about capos is that you can use the same chord shapes you're already comfortable playing, but it comes out in a different key. Several makers offer small, lightweight ukulele capos in a variety of colors, with some of the most popular being the Kyser Quick-Change ($19.95), D'Addario Ukulele Pro ($19.95), Shubb L-9 ($17.95), and G7th UltraLight ($14.99).

PICKS

Sure, fingers are great for playing, but a pick can offer more volume and clarity for strumming or picking single-note parts than are available from your fingers' flesh and nails. The astounding variety of materials and shapes available can also offer you many different sounds that you might find useful. Plastic or nylon flatpicks can sound harsh on ukulele strings, so ukulele players tend to favor the warmer, fuller sound of flatpicks made from softer materials like felt or leather, or they might use fingers and a plastic thumbpick. Some of Hawaii's greatest players, including Herb Ohta, Jr. and Bryan Tolentino, don't leave home without a thumbpick, and for about a dollar, you can get a thumbpick from Dunlop or Fred Kelly. Flatpicks made from soft felt or felt-like materials are available from D'Addario, Dunlop, and Martin, and strap-maker Sherrin's Threads offers leather picks. Each material gives you a different sound and feel, so experimentation is not only fun, it won't cost much.

SLIDES

Some of the most soul-stirring music ever played or recorded came from the sound of a slide gliding across guitar strings. But there is no reason why guitarists should have all of the fun to themselves, and while slide ukulele is pretty niche, it can be worth checking out for the curious player. Playing slide takes practice, but it unlocks all of the expressive, emotive notes that can happen between the frets—plus playing slide looks great onstage. Slide players delight in the different sounds offered by different materials, and while you can use just about any hard and smooth surface, from pocket knives to animal bones or beer bottles for a slide, the most common slides are made from glass or metal tubes and fit over a ring or pinky finger. Glass slides tend to give a smoother tone, while chrome and brass slides are usually a little heavier, with a crisper, brighter tone. Some of the easiest-to-find and most affordable glass and metal slides are from D'Addario (starting at $6.99), Dunlop ($6.61), and Ernie Ball ($4.99). A small cost for the fun and challenge of playing slide. *u*

TO STRAP OR NOT STRAP?

That is one question every ukulele player will face

BY HEIDI SWEDBERG

For years, I didn't use a strap on my ukulele. Why on earth would I need one on such a tiny thing? The uke wants to be clutched close to the heart, not strung on a rope. I sang and strummed without a care.

Everything changed the day I went to take Daniel Ward's first flamenco ukulele workshop at McCabe's, the legendary guitar store in Santa Monica, California. Apparently, the world was not ready; nobody else came— which made me the luckiest girl on earth: I got a private lesson in *sevillanas*, fingerstyle melodies, and sharp rhythmic patterns from the traditional Spanish guitar repertoire. Within the hour, I realized, "Oh my G C E A, I need a strap!"

Some see this as a divisive uke moment, but don't let high- (or low-) G anxiety get to you. If you're wondering whether it's time for you to button up and strap on, here are some honest answers and easy guidelines.

PAUL HEMMINGS   New York, NY

"Most ukulele straps I find are too thin, and if you try to use a guitar strap, it's usually too bulky. I've got the Goldilocks ukulele strap because it's just right. I set the strap so that the instrument is in the same position, regardless of whether I'm sitting or standing—I usually practice sitting down—and I recommend Goldilocks straps to students for the same reason."

CATHY FINK   Silver Spring, MD

"Using a strap means that neither of your hands are responsible for holding your uke in the perfect position. Many players, especially beginners, use the left hand to hold up the neck and the right hand to squeeze the uke in place. The strap takes care of that so both hands can be focused on playing."

DANIEL WARD   Los Angeles, CA

"Liz Olney designed and made all my straps. They're pretty swanky, but the core design is what makes it for me. The 3/4-inch width seems perfect for ukulele—balance is uniform, and the soft backing means no slipping at the shoulder.

"A strap allows both hands to move freely with no forced support of the instrument. Try and play a single-note melody on the open strings without a strap while standing, and feel where you end up compromising to hold up the instrument. For concert and tenor sizes, it really helps.

"I do pick up ukes without a strap all the time. When material is not difficult or I'm just strumming on a little soprano at a jam, it's great fun."

ANDY ANDREWS   Puna, HI

"Never have and I hope I never will. I play nothing but a standard size, which makes them manageable to hold. (I do play tenor sax, and I use a strap then!) I like my hands to be dancing across the top of the uke. Holding down a chord with my left hand, palm against the neck, keeps it place, and the gravity of up and down strums keeps it floating in mid-air in front of me.

"Without a strap, the instrument is moveable. I find that when I'm playing a B♭ chord, I hold the instrument with the headstock pointing straight away from me, whereas on 'double bar' chords [i.e., m7♭5] I have to pull the instrument flat against my body. With different strums, I hold it differently, too—higher for fingerpicking, lower for a Pete Townshend rock strum, and I like to change it up during a song."

"Like a violin, a lot of sound comes off the back of the instrument, and if you are using a strap, the instrument nestles down into your gut, and you lose it all. And, if you're wearing a strap, you can't spin it around like Roy Smeck."

BARRY PRUDHOMME Ontario, Canada
"I have always played with a strap, as I need all my fingers to pick. This ukulele is a Mya-Moe tenor with Clint Eastwood's "Man with No Name" character—featured in director Sergio Leone's "Dollars" trilogy—inlaid on the fretboard; the corresponding strap was made by Terry Misner, owner of Action Custom Straps. He has made all my straps that match my other ukuleles."

TAMMY ST. PIERRE   Traverse City, MI
"It is nice to be able to let go of the uke and walk around to talk to people at uke group. I bought a white Kala arch-top ukulele so I could change the color of my straps to match an outfit, special occasion, or holiday."

MARSHA GRESSO   Interlochen, MI
"When I first bought my ukulele in Hawaii, I didn't get a strap because I wasn't sure I wanted to have someone drill a hole into my koa uke. But I found it difficult to hold, and I got tired easily. I purchased an adjustable strap that had a J-hook clip-on, but it felt clumsy and my uke didn't feel secure and safe as I moved around. When I returned to Hawaii and the shop where I bought my ukulele, I had the owner install a strap button. I also think it sounds better when I'm not clutching it tightly."

WHAT A STRAP CAN DO FOR YOU

- Help keep your instrument in an optimum position
- Allow your right and left hands to play more freely
- Give you confidence and independence of movement
- Present opportunities for fun accessorizing and gifting

BUTTON UP!

Ready for a strap? Some straps don't require buttons, but most do. You can take your instrument to a respected shop and have strap buttons installed, but it's not a difficult job to tackle at home if you have a few tools and some courage. Follow these instructions from Elderly Instrument's head repair tech, Joe Konkoly:

A Here's everything you need: strap, strap buttons with felt washers to protect the instrument, fine drill bit, Phillips head screw bit, and a hand drill.

B Take a look at the bottom of your instrument, known as the tailblock: That's where the first button will go. Use a ruler to mark the midpoint of the center joint.

C Gently drill the pilot hole.

D Screw the button in.

E You will need another button on the neck heel, unless you opt to attach your strap to your headstock underneath the strings. For many, the choice between a strap on the neck heel or headstock is a question of balance and comfort. Lay your instrument upside down on a padded surface (a towel or carpet square) and locate and mark the location for the button on the treble side of the neck heel. Gently drill at an angle about 1/4-inch into the wood. (Note the solid "sweet spot" where the button goes in.)

F Screw in the strap button.

G Put strap on buttons, adjust length to your liking. Voila! Go forth and conquer!

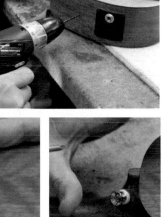

HAPPY TRAILS TO UKE

Tips to keep your ukulele safe and sound while traveling

BY AARON KEIM

In summer or year 'round, it's hard to beat the thrill of packing up the ol' uke and hitting the road to make some musical memories! After all, its portability is one of the things that makes the ukulele perfect for any party or adventure. Before you take off, I'll share a few tips to keep your ukulele safe and sound while traveling.

From years of repair experience, I need to share precautions with you about the three most common travel-related repairs I've seen. First: A ukulele left in a car in the heat. Even a mild sunny day can quickly lead to glue-melting temperatures in a car. Always bring your instrument with you, even if you are heading into a restaurant. It's easy to tell when a uke has had a heat-related event because of common effects such as loose binding, open seams, loose braces, and warped tops. Second: If you are going to leave your ukulele on a chair while you go get another drink, just know that someone could sit on it. Believe it or not, it happens all the time! I have fixed many ukes that accidentally were sat on and it's not a cheap or easy fix. Third: If you are going to put your ukulele in its case or gig bag, close the latches or zipper it up. I've seen many ukes tumble to the ground because someone picked up a case by the handle with the top unlatched. Latch it up, even if you are coming right back.

Speaking of cases, should you bring a hardshell case or gig bag on your trip? I have taken both around the world and like each for different reasons. A gig bag with backpack straps makes walking through the airport easy and you can add other carry-on items in the pockets. But keep in mind that a gig bag will lose a fight with someone else's roller suitcase if slammed in an overhead compartment! A hardshell case with a shoulder strap is a good compromise and is my standard carry.

Which leads us to flying with your uke, which I do many times per year. First of all, no matter what size case you are using, insist that you keep it with you in the cabin. It's really the best way to keep it safe, and the law is on your side (see sidebar).

Airlines are permitted to decide if your instrument counts toward your number of carry-on items, so check the airline's policy before leaving home. When I travel with my family, we usually just carry on an instrument and a small tote bag each; we always check our suitcases so we can keep our ukes close. The head flight attendant, and the captain, of course, are really in charge of what comes in the cabin. The gate agent or ticket agent is not really the decider, so try to wait to plead your case until you get into the cabin. Make friends with the flight attendants, because sometimes you can convince them to let you stash an instrument in the crew coat closet, in the gap behind the last row of first class, or other "secret" spots. Watch for overhead bins that already have strange-sized items in there instead of normal rolling bags. You can often add your uke to double-up with other odd-sized items.

And then there's the eternal question: which uke to bring? I often hear from customers that they take a cheap uke when they travel because they are scared to bring their handmade instrument out in the world. I understand that, but it also makes me sad because ukuleles are made to be played, after all. As long as you are careful, having your favorite uke on adventures with you will only serve to improve the overall experience. Yes, some adventures, like rafting trips, call for a plastic ukulele like an Outdoor Ukulele, but I prefer a wooden uke while on the road. What about maintenance? A few simple items slipped in your case are good insurance: an extra set of strings, a small screwdriver for adjusting tuning pegs, nail file and nail clippers, and a humidifier are key. I also add a small musical notebook and my phone for making digital recordings and I'm ready to hit the road! *u*

HELPING HANDS

Top players discuss the sometimes overlooked subject of hand and nail care
BY HEIDI SWEDBERG

Music is made up of two basic components: pitch and rhythm, and for the most part, these fundamentals are divided between the chording and the "speaking" hand. For 90 percent of us (with apologies to the left-handed 10 percent), the right hand is all about rhythm.

Fingerstyle playing, picking, and strumming techniques unique to each player are often reflected in their most intimate tool: their nails. Manicures are not just for the pampered. Musicians' fingernail requirements are very specific and often have little to do with visual aesthetics.

The first thing you might notice about a string player's manicure is that it is lopsided. Most serious players have very short nails on their chording hands. As a result, chording hands often look alike. The right hand, however, is where things get crazy.

The manicure on a ukulele player's picking hand can tell you a lot about how they play. Today's top players bring a wide variety of styles to the ukulele: Hawaiian, classical, vintage swing, jazz, pop, folk, reggae, and flamenco. Here, the ukulele's right-hand women and men share the long and short of their rhythm styles and manicure strategies.

HAWAIIAN-STYLE

Hawaiian-style playing combines fingerstyle melodies and strumming. These two players use the pinky finger to stabilize their right hands against the instrument, and pick mostly with index and middle fingers. The thumbnail is a powerful tool, often kept a little longer.

BRYAN TOLENTINO
"With my acrylic nails, I get more articulation that bites through amplified music when I'm performing on stage. When I get my nails done, I tell them 'thicker than normal' for added strength. I usually file down my two nails (index and middle) as they get longer."

HERB OHTA, JR.
"Shorter is better, but sometimes I grow them out. Don't use nail-strengthening products on your nails; your nail needs to breathe. Instead, take gelatin tablets or eat a lot of Jell-O."

CLASSICAL

Uke players with a background in classical playing are often first schooled on guitar and develop a strong feel for the string and a keen awareness of tone.

MIM

"I took classical guitar lessons in high school, so a lot of my picking comes from that background. In an ideal world, I would have longer nails that have a bit of an offset curve filed into them, but then I would have to stop sanding saddles, playing in the dirt, and loading donkeys. Being a rabid nail biter, it took me about two years to train myself just to bite my left hand."

DANI JOY

"I take the classical-guitar approach where I use the *p i m a* (thumb, index, middle, and ring fingers, respectively) of my right hand. I find it useful to have nails that are just long enough to clip the strings. I have '*i m a*' acrylic additions—with pinky and thumb natural. I notice a lot of people who have a long thumbnail for picking and tremolos. I'm going to try that at my next appointment. I need strong nails that won't shred after one set, and also offer more volume with less effort. Most nail salons don't shave the top surface down enough, leaving me with chunky acrylic that deadens my sound. Density doesn't seem to work so good—I suppose that's why guitar picks are so thin."

DANIEL HO

"I studied classical guitar, and both my left- and right-hand technique are in the classical-guitar style. I keep my nails as short as possible so I can feel the strings with my fingertips. I have a lot more control and power with shorter nails, and I don't break them as often. The shape just follows the tips of my fingers. I file them a little bit every day to keep them at precisely the right length."

FLAMENCO

Traditional flamenco techniques are so detailed and varied, they require a lifetime of study and a hand of fully armored nails.

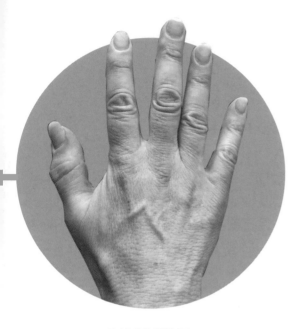

DANIEL WARD

"I file each nail differently so it hits the string at the best angle for my hand and gets the smoothest tone. For me, that's fairly flat in the middle (but at an angle) and rounded on the sides, so the string is plucked right where the flesh and the nail meet. I file them constantly. Even the nail edge is rounded, so the string can connect and 'roll' around the nail. I keep the thumbnail longer so I can use fast flamenco techniques like *alzapúa* (cross-string flips), double bouncing, and a type of sweep picking.

"I would break a nail in the first 30 seconds of playing without my acrylic 'armor.' Even the pinky, as I strum with the backs of the nails, too. My ukulele needs tap plates to keep me from putting holes in the wood—so, don't let me play your uke! I will scratch it unless I'm careful."

JAZZ & POP

The province of individualists: strum it, swing it, and bring it!

CASEY MACGILL

"My nails are short because I also play the piano. I prefer short nails. Really long nails creep me out. If I play a lot, my strumming will break my fingernail, even though it's short, so I go to a nail salon and get a clear false nail painted on top of my index fingernail. My strumming is almost always a straight swing strum, downstrokes with my index finger, and occasional accents with upstrokes from my thumb (nail). For softer volume and texture, I use the fleshy part of my thumb for downstrokes, instead."

SARAH MAISEL

"My nails are all about the same length—1/16-inch past my actual fingertip. This allows me to just clip the string with the nail, to allow the pad of my finger to be most of what hits the string. My thumbnail is a tad longer—maybe 1/8-inch past my fingertip. They are my natural nails and I feel very fortunate to have very strong nails.

"I notice any time I put nail polish on, it changes my tone when I strum. I also will totally wreck a nice manicure, so it's just a waste of money."

CRAIG CHEE

"I used to have all of my nails at a decent length, but eventually fell in love with a mellower tone created by keeping my fingernails short to the tip. Getting a really warm tone was much harder with longer nails. My thumbnail is just a hair longer so that I can get a very solid note on the way down (hitting both my thumb tip and nail) and have a nice solid hit on the way up using the longer nail. This is how many of us can get that very fast thumb speed up and down."

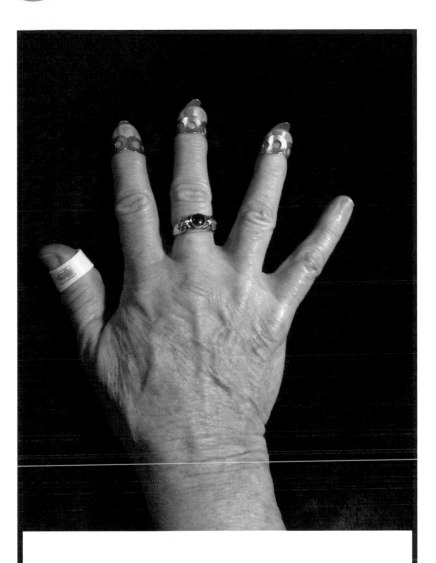

RESONATOR ROGUE
Don't try this at home, kids!

DEL REY
"I feel like what I'm doing is a really bad thing to encourage . . . I am getting a good sound out of it, but mostly people don't.

"When I first started playing ukulele with the Yes Yes Boys (stand-up bass, washboard, sax, and clarinet), I tried bare fingers—blood on the frets. I tried acrylics: Have you read up on those chemicals? Nasty! So I started using the same picks I use on guitar, with a smaller thumb pick. I've gained the volume and crispness I like, but I've given up down-strokes—so all the classic ukulele strumming techniques and rhythm strokes are out. It takes a lot of practice to turn force into sweet sound instead of pick noise. In most instances, a musician's time would be better spent playing bare-fingered. I often play without picks for fun and pleasure, when I'm just enjoying the instrument for its own sake."

NAIL-CARE TOOLS THEY CAN'T LIVE WITHOUT

CRAIG CHEE AND SARAH MAISEL
"We love our nail clipper—it's from Japan, the brand is Green Bell, and it's the sharpest and smoothest nail clipper we've ever had."

DANIEL WARD "Super-glue and baking soda for repairs—the flamenco speedball."

MIM "My best friend sends me a container of hand cream from Lush every year for my birthday. I am stingy, so I just use a little bit when I realize my hands have gone downhill, and I make it last all year until my birthday rolls around again."

HERB OHTA, JR. "Glass files."

BRYAN TOLENTINO "Jake [Shimabukuro] turned me on to Nail Sandpaper, but you can only get it in Japan!"

DANIEL HO "When I record, I use foam blocks with four very-fine sandpapers."

BUZZ PATROL
Finding and fixing buzzes and rattles
BY AARON KEIM

Tapping the front and back should resonate like a drum. If you hear a rattle or crack, you may have a loose brace.

Aaron Keim

Every time I arrive to teach and perform at a festival, people come to me with problems regarding their ukes. They are frustrated with a funny buzz, a rattle, or a sour note, and have hit a wall after reading conflicting advice on too many forums and online searches. Dealing with these undesirable sounds is pretty common, but it doesn't have to be a big deal. Let's talk about some common causes and what you can do to fix them.

First, let's set the stage. The typical ukulele is a strange collage of wood, metal, plastic, and bone, with each material expanding and contracting at its own rate with the weather. They are built to close tolerances to sound great and play easily, but the difference of a few thousands of an inch can throw things off and make for a buzz.

I have seen it in high-end customs and mail-order cheapies. It just happens. But, before you even worry about your uke, you need to worry about your strumming- and fretting-hand technique. Poor fretting and clumsy picking will make any uke buzz! You may want to ask a friend to play your uke and see if they have the same problem. After that, you may consider the many possibilities we will discuss below. Yes, there are several things you can check and fix yourself, but be prepared to take your uke to a professional repair person who works on acoustic instruments. Which is worse—getting frustrated trying to research the problem and do it yourself, or spending the $75 for one hour of a pro's time?

Before you hit the shop, you should check the following, in this order.

1. ACCESSORIES

A clip-on tuner or a plastic part of your strap can rattle. Remove those accessories first to check if it is causing a buzz. Also, a button on a cuff on your right arm can rattle, so push up your sleeve.

2. HARDWARE

Sometimes a screw or nut will loosen on your tuning peg, strap button, or endpin jack. If it seems like one of them is buzzing, touch your hand to it while you pluck the string to see if it dampens the vibration. If needed, you can use a screwdriver or wrench to tighten them. Take care to use the right tool so that you don't strip screwheads or round over nuts.

3. STRINGS

Did you recently change to a new set of strings? Different makes and models of strings have different diameters (or gauges), so you may have a string sitting in a slot that is too big for it. More commonly, your strings are old and worn, with frayed or flat spots causing a buzz. Changing to a new set may solve the problem.

4. PICKUP WIRES

The inside wires of your pickup (if you have one) can creep over to lightly touch the top, causing them to rattle. You may be able to reach in and push them over. If there is a lot of loose cable, you can add a small self-adhesive clip designed for keeping computer cords out of the way. Just place it inside the uke through the sound hole, on the inside waist of the instrument.

Loose cables can be held in place with a small adhesive clip.

Checking for the most common cause of buzzes, high frets.

5. A LOOSE OR BROKEN BRACE

This is a more significant issue that a pro will have to fix. You can tell if this is the problem by tapping with your finger on the outside of the uke on the front and back. The tap should resonate like a drum, if it makes a dry crack or rattle sound, then a brace is likely cracked or unglued. A loose brace can cause the top to warp or the bridge to twist, as well—it's pretty serious and needs attention from a pro.

6. HIGH FRETS

The absolute most common cause of a buzz is a high fret or frets. This could be just one note on your uke buzzing, or it could be several notes on one string in a row. Even if your uke had no high frets when it left the shop, they could develop over time with changes in temperature and humidity. More commonly, the high frets were there all along, but you didn't notice in your first few years of playing while you were learning to play. You may have noticed the buzz only when you started playing up the neck, fingerpicking, and playing single-note melodies.

To fix this, a luthier must find the high frets with a small straightedge, tap or file them down, crown their tops round again, and polish them smooth—a process called "dressing" the frets. Sometimes this takes just a few minutes, sometimes it takes a lot of work, especially if your instrument's neck is warped or twisted. Even a high-quality instrument from a professional luthier or factory may need a little fret dressing after a couple of years. Just consider it a 1,000-mile checkup.

Filing down a high fret.

7. STRING HEIGHT

The last thing to ask your luthier about is the string height at the nut and saddle. In my opinion, most factory-made ukuleles have the strings too high at the nut and too low at the saddle. This makes them hard to play and prone to buzzing. Strings vibrate in a wave-like shape and need plenty of room at the 12th fret to vibrate. Even if your frets have been dressed, the strings will buzz if the saddle is too low.

But who to take your instrument to? I really need to stress that you should take it to someone who specializes in acoustic instruments. At some big "rock 'n' roll" guitar shops, there is still a prejudice against the ukulele, and they may not give you the attention you deserve. Ask your most experienced local friends who they trust. If that doesn't work, search online for the right local luthier. It may even be someone you find through social media who is running a small home shop.

One final thing to consider. I often find people overly concerned and obsessed with tiny noises coming out of their uke. If I want to, I can make any uke buzz at any fret if I pick it a certain way.

Think about this: Is the noise coming through in the music and noticeable to the audience? Or am I overthinking this late at night on the couch by myself? Hopefully, taking these steps will help to get your uke back in "strumming order" as soon as possible. *u*

COMMON SENSE CARE

How to keep your ukulele in tip-top shape

BY MIM

Mim at the workbench

What does your ukulele want from you? It wants to be played, it wants to be enjoyed, and it wants to be cared for. So, let's talk about the last part—how best to care for your new ukulele friend!

CLEANING

If you are playing your ukulele as you should, your hands are all over it. Hands are dirty and oily. My advice is to keep a soft microfiber cloth in your ukulele case and go ahead and wipe it down after a long playing session. If you get a buildup of grime, a slightly damp microfiber cloth should do the trick. You can use a little bit of polish on a gloss finish, but use a light hand and don't *over* polish, as this can leave swirl marks. It is important that there is no debris on your cloth. Satin and matte finishes require different care. You do not want to use polish, because it will seep into the wood and it can change the sheen of your ukulele and leave it splotchy. For those finishes it is best to just stick with a cloth.

I like to change my strings a few times a year, and that is when I take a moment and spend some time really giving my fretboard a good once over. With the strings removed, it is easy to clean off any debris before

It is important to be aware of the temperature and humidity wherever your ukes are kept.

treating it with a fretboard oil of your choice. There are many specifically made for fretboards, and a small bottle should last you a long time. Just remember, a little goes a long way. Rub any excess oil off your fretboard before re-stringing.

TUNERS AND HARDWARE

A few times a year, I take note of the hardware on my ukulele. If my tuners are held on with a nut, it is always good to ensure they are tightened. With a lot of play they can sometimes come loose and create a slight metallic buzz, often leading players to think there is a bigger problem, when all they need to do is tighten the nut or adjust the screw on the end of the tuner knob. If your ukulele has friction tuners and they are no longer holding tune, take a Phillips head screwdriver and tighten the screw on the back of the tuner until you reach your preferred tension.

STRINGS

Strings are not meant to last forever. They are made to stretch into tune, and eventually they will be stretched too thin and need to be replaced. I am often asked how often strings need to be replaced. It depends on how long you play, how aggressively you play, and what kind of strings you use. (For more, see "Things About Strings" on page 28.)

TEMPERATURE

This may seem obvious, but you should avoid subjecting your ukulele to extreme temperatures. Leaving your ukulele in an extreme hot or cold environment can cause damage. Leaving your ukulele in a hot car can dry out the wood and loosen glue joints. It would be best for the instrument to be stored in the trunk, but better yet, it should be taken inside. Similarly, extreme cold can

also damage an instrument. Always keep in mind that a sudden change in temperature rather than a gradual warm-up or cool-down can be harmful. If your ukulele has been out in the cold, allow it to warm up to room temperature inside the case before exposing it to the warm air. This will minimize the chance that the sudden temperature shift could leave small cracks in the ukulele's finish.

HUMIDITY

The Oasis OH-32 ukulele humidifier is made from a special fabric that allows water vapor, but not water, to pass through it. As more humidity is needed, the Humigel crystals release it, creating a vacuum that shrinks the humidifier and lets you see when it needs to be refilled.

Humidity, the amount of water vapor in the air, is my number one concern when it comes to ukuleles. It is the hardest issue to tackle, because it is always in a constant state of flux. Wood reacts to humidity, and most ukuleles are made out of wood. The sweet spot for ukuleles is generally between 45 and 55 percent humidity. The "danger zone" is when your ukulele sits in humidity lower than 35 percent or higher than 65 percent.

When humidity is too low, ukulele symptoms may include:

- **Sharp fret ends**: As the fretboard shrinks, it exposes the fret ends.
- **Fret buzz**: Your fretboard may shrink and bow backwards, making the neck relief inadequate and lowering the action to the point where the strings will hit the frets.
- **Structural damage and cracks**: Braces can loosen, sides can pull away from the body, and the wood can separate, causing cracks if the ukulele has a sudden drop in humidity or is allowed to remain in a dry environment.

When the humidity level is too high, ukulele symptoms may include:

- **Structural damage**: The wood can swell, causing bows to the soundboard, and even loosening glue joints.
- **High action**: The neck may bow upwards, raising the string action and compromising the playability.
- **Corrosion**: It can lead to corrosion of the frets and other metal components on your ukulele.

The most common damage I see is from low humidity. An extreme humidity change does more damage than a slow and gradual change. Many of these issues can be repaired by a skilled technician, but it is always better to not have to repair your ukulele in the first place.

There is not a one size-fits-all humidity solution for all of my customers. They all come from drastically different climates. In my state of Virginia alone there are five different climate zones that would lend themselves to different humidity levels and fluctuations. The Big Island of Hawaii boasts eight climate zones. My advice is:

- **Know your climate.** If you live in the dry desert of Phoenix, Arizona, your humidity needs are going to be very different from someone who lives in the Florida Keys.

- **Know your seasons**. In the mountains of Virginia, I have to run humidifiers all winter. But when the summer hits, the weather is very humid, so I actually have to run a dehumidifier.

- **Know how climate and seasons affect your indoor humidity.** This can be easily done with a humidity gauge from a hardware store. Make sure you are aware of the indoor humidity during all seasons, and how it is affected when using different methods of temperature control in your home. Wood heat tends to dry the air. Air conditioning can also dry the air, but some systems re-introduce humidity back into the environment, so it is best to track your individual home.

- **Consider a case.** When humidity levels are extreme, it might be best to keep your ukulele in the case and track the humidity there. It is a lot easier to purchase or make a small ukulele humidifier and control the humidity in a case, rather than a whole room. There are a lot of hygrometers for ukulele cases that can let you know if your ukulele is resting in "comfortable" humidity inside its case. Since I run an ukulele shop, I have ukuleles on my wall, but in the winter I have two five-gallon humidifiers running to keep my humidity levels ideal. They cycle on and off most days, but on brutally cold days and extremely dry days, my shop has constant fan noise. This would not be ideal for a home.

- **Be prepared.** Instead of having to repair a problem, head off any humidity damage by purchasing a hygrometer and a humidifier. It is a cheap and easy way to have peace of mind. You can also make one of your own. Just make sure no humidifiers come in direct contact with the wood of your ukulele.

It is well known that laminate ukuleles are less prone to damage as humidity fluctuates. But keep in mind they still should not be exposed to extreme humidity levels. Their fretboards are often made out of wood, and therefore they are still susceptible to sharp fret ends and neck-relief damage if allowed to remain in an extremely dry or moist environment.

After this humidity discussion, I do not want you to think ukuleles are high-maintenance and delicate. Once you get the knack for your personal humidity levels, it usually is as simple as remembering to refill your case humidifier once a week. Many people live in milder climates where this may never be an issue, but I would rather err on the side of caution than to not warn about a potential problem. Also, even if you live in a mild climate where humidity is not a concern, you may travel with your ukulele to a different climate and it is better to have too much information than not enough.

THE CASE QUESTION

One final thing to consider is what kind of case to choose. Case preference often comes down to lifestyle, climate, and your own personal taste. I will share some thoughts that might be helpful when making that decision—but understand there is no right or wrong answer.

When considering the case that will house your ukulele, think about the functionality of the case, the climate, and your travel. If you travel frequently, need a lot of humidity control, are clumsy, or have a lot of activity around your home, a hard case might be preferable. It will seal the ukulele inside making it easier to control the humidity level, while also protecting your ukulele from outside forces. That being said, if you do a lot of travel that includes walking, you may want to consider a structured soft-case or well-padded gig bag with backpack straps. You will get a lot of protection and it will make travel with your ukulele a little more comfortable and less inhibitive when you have the option of *wearing* your instrument. Simple gig bags are an affordable way to protect your ukulele. They are preferable if you do not live in an extreme climate, own a laminate ukulele, or have a home that does not experience humidity fluctuations or clumsy chaos.

ENJOY YOUR UKULELE

This article presents a lot of information. But the most important advice I can give you is to love your ukulele. Play the music you like to play. Do not get hung up on perfection, but rather make music that makes you happy. Then when you are ready, share that music with those around you! *u*

THE DANCE OF THE JUMPING FLEA

The evolution of the ukulele

BY MICHAEL WRIGHT

History has dealt the ukulele an unusual hand that's full of contradictions. It sways seductively to an undulating hula, or jumps to the Charleston with arms and legs akimbo. It lubricates boisterous college students at parties and teaches little children how to count time in music class. In the hands of a very young child, it's a charming toy that elicits chortles of amusement; in the hands of a virtuoso it's a demanding concert solo instrument that commands standing ovations.

Honolulu, 1899

GUITARS ON THE IBERIAN PENINSULA

Conflicting associations have been part of the ukulele story ever since the figure-8-shaped Spanish guitar appeared in what's now northwestern Spain as a politico-religious reaction to the Arabic lute (l'oud) of the Islamic occupation. There were four-stringed guitars that mainly accompanied fandangos—folk dancing and singing—and six-course vihuelas that played composed polyphonic music. Guitars slowly spread southward and became a Spanish cultural symbol during the *reconquista*.

As guitars evolved there were numerous variations in shape and size, some of which went extinct over time and some of which settled down into obscure corners of the world. A glimpse of this diversity can still be seen in the many regional Portuguese guitars (Braguesa, Beiroa, Amerantina, Toeira, etc.) that remained in use well into the 20th century. Indeed, it was a pair of these Portuguese guitar-byways that found refuge on the island of Madeira and became the modern ukulele.

GUITARS COME TO THE ATLANTIC ISLANDS

Madeira is the main island in a small archipelago in the North Atlantic Ocean about 430 miles west off the coast of Morocco. Funchal is its capital and largest city. In around 1420, the Portuguese annexed and settled Madeira as part of their Voyages of Discovery.

European explorers were ever on the lookout for suitable places to cultivate sugar cane, and by the mid-15th century, Madeira had become the first of many sugar plantations that sprouted in the wake of Portuguese caravels and Spanish galleons.

The Portuguese also transplanted music into Madeira, including two guitars—the machete and the rajão. The machete, originally from the northern Portugal city of Braga (and called the braguinho or cavaquinho), is a diminutive guitar about the size of a soprano ukulele, featuring four metal wire strings tuned to an open G chord, from bass to treble D G B D (the same as the stopped strings of the modern 5-string banjo). The machete accompanied songs sung—somewhat crudely, according to tourist reports—by everyone all over Madeira.

Visitor accounts also describe more refined performances heard in Funchal. This may also have been on a machete, but details make it more likely to have been on the rajão. Bigger and slightly more elongated than the machete, the rajão sported five gut strings tuned G G C E A, in the

Madeiran musicians with rajão and machete, forbears of the ukulele.

same intervals as a Spanish guitar, in fourths with a third between the second and third strings. However, the fourth and fifth strings are tuned an octave *higher* than a guitar would be, so the lowest string is the third string, yielding what's called "reentrant" tuning.

Sugar remained Madeira's principal cash crop until cheaper cane grown in Brazil and the Caribbean replaced it during the 16th and 17th centuries, after which the island switched to wine making. But sugar would also play a major role in the ukulele story on another island chain on the opposite side of the world from Madeira in the Pacific Ocean—the Hawaiian Islands. Situated almost right in the center of the Pacific, halfway between North America and China, Hawaii would become a vital way station once international whaling and trade moved into the Pacific in the 19th century.

GUITARS COME TO THE PACIFIC ISLANDS

The modern era in Hawaii began when the English Captain James Cook made his first landfall in 1778. On a visit in 1793, Captain George Vancouver presented a gift of five cows and a bull to King Kamehameha I ("The Great"). Kamehameha turned the cattle loose, protecting them with a *tabu*. It didn't take long for the cows to multiply and create a big problem!

Foreign marksmen were hired to cull the wild cow herds in the early 1800s, but in 1832 three cowboys from Mexican California were brought in to help control the cattle. They corralled rather than shot them, thus preserving their hides and turning Hawaiian beef and beef products into a major trade asset for acquiring imported goods.

Mexican cowboys were known as *paniolas* (from "*espaniola*," meaning "from Spain"). Many writers hypothesize that, since Spanish guitars were present throughout Mexico, the *paniolas* must have introduced guitars into Hawaii. There is no evidence for this. However, there were many other possible routes, including ongoing direct trade with Mexico and the rising tide of sailors. What *is* certain is that an advertisement in *The Polynesian* magazine from June 6, 1840, offered guitar strings for sale, so enough guitars were present in Hawaii at that time to justify promoting accessories.

In any case, California *did* make another indirect contribution to guitars coming to Hawaii. In January of 1848, a month before that part of Mexico became a U.S. Territory, an employee of John Sutter (who coincidentally employed Hawaiians to work his farm), was building a new sawmill when he saw something glistening in the mill race. By the next year the California Gold Rush was in high gear.

Right behind the gold prospectors were the provisioners, and after them the entertainers. However, you could only see a trick horse-riding act or a pretty chanteuse so many times. As audiences declined, performers looked for new places to go after San Francisco. The answer became the Pacific Circuit: Tahiti, Yokohama, Shanghai, New Zealand, Australia . . . and Honolulu. During the 1850s, American entertainers became regulars on Honolulu stages, with performances including one of the top theatrical forms of the day—minstrelsy,

to which guitars and banjos were fundamental.

Guitar playing became something of a fad in Honolulu in the 1860s, but it wasn't until the 1870s that guitars and banjos seem to have infiltrated the nation's many singing clubs and orchestras.

THE POLITICS OF SUGAR

Whatever path guitars took to get to Hawaii, they arrived at the beginning of a political maelstrom that involved sugar. The first Puritan Christian missionaries from New England began evangelizing there in around 1820. Essential to their gospel toolbox was spreading the Word through music, primarily hymn singing. It's highly unlikely that they ever employed guitars. In any case, native Hawaiians warmly embraced Western-style music and quickly became accomplished at it.

While the missionaries viewed Hawaii as perfect fields for harvesting souls for the Lord, their children quickly recognized Hawaii as a perfect place to harvest fields of sugar

cane. In the 1830s, the great sugar plantations were established and along with them the *haole* (non-native residents, usually, but not always, Americans) sugar barons. These businessmen increasingly viewed Hawaii as their own possession and set in motion events that would lead to the overthrow of the monarchy, establishment of the Hawaiian Republic, and eventually its annexation as an American Territory in 1898–1900.

However, it wasn't the political machinations of the *haole* sugar barons, but their employment needs, that would create the ukulele. The sugar barons expected to make their fortunes using native labor to provide the blood, sweat, and tears. But the barons constantly complained that the Hawaiians were "too lazy." Plus, exposure to foreign diseases wreaked havoc on the native Hawaiian population, causing it to shrink dramatically. More and "better" workers were required to meet the demand. In 1852, the sugar barons began importing Chinese laborers, followed by the

H-26   Cutting Sugar Cane, Hawaiian Islands.

first Japanese workers in the late 1860s. Madeirans would soon follow.

However, the first known Madeirans to work the cane fields did not arrive with that intention. Instead they were the marooned crew of a Madeiran whaling ship that had been inadvertently sunk by the Confederate cruiser *Shenandoah* in 1865 at the end of the Civil War. They got jobs on a large sugar plantation and became famous in the vicinity for the spirited playing of their machetes (the little guitars, not the sharp knives!). These sailors had no direct part in the ukulele story, but they *are* credited with being the first to strum metal-stringed guitars in Hawaii. The introduction of wire strings would have an enormous impact on the subsequent development of Hawaiian steel guitar.

GUITARS TRAVEL FROM MADEIRA TO HAWAII

Back in Madeira, times were not so good. Beginning in the 1830s famine and poverty increasingly plagued Madeirans, setting off numerous successive waves of emigration to the Americas. The immigrants carried their machetes and rajãos with them and they eventually transformed into other Latin American instruments.

In the mid-1870s, the Hawaiian government published a recruitment brochure touting the pleasures of living in the Islands and dispatched representatives across the globe to entice more cane labor. When they got to Madeira, their pitch was not a hard sell. Hundreds of desperate Madeirans—for whom working sugar cane was not an entirely alien notion—agreed to sail to Hawaii as "contract workers" and ply the

Native Hawaiians playing ukulele and taropatch.

fields for a three-year term. The first Portuguese-speaking contract workers from Madeira arrived in Honolulu in 1878, one of them singing and playing a machete as they docked. More than 25,000 would eventually heed the call. The second cohort arrived in August of 1879 and included Manuel Nunes, Augusto Dias, and Jose do Espirito Santo, three cabinet makers who would become prominent Hawaiian ukulele- and guitar-makers. Literally within days of the Madeirans' debarking, Honolulu newspapers were reporting that that these new immigrants were hanging out on street corners playing music.

The machete and rajão couldn't have arrived at a more fortuitous time. Both the missionaries and their sugar baron children were approaching the apex of their power. Traditional Hawaiian culture was greatly disparaged as being pagan and licentious. Growing restraints were imposed upon royal constitutional autonomy. *Haole* forces were

working to draw Hawaii ever closer into the sphere of United States influence. Enter King David Kalakaua (1836–1891).

In 1874, the last direct descendant of Kamehameha I died and David Kalakaua was elected as his successor. King Kalakaua was highly educated, a poet and composer who played guitar and ukulele, among other instruments. He encouraged Western culture. Honolulu echoed with the plays of Shakespeare and Italian opera. But he also revived some of the old ways, the ancient chants and poetry known as *mele oli* (a capella) and *mele hula* dancing (accompanied).

But even more importantly, Kalakaua encouraged the *blending* of traditional Hawaiian and modern Western culture. Ancient instruments such as nose flutes that once had accompanied the hula were replaced by guitars and later, ukuleles as "*hula kui*" or new hula. Old melodies found their way into modern music.

HAWAIIANS CREATE THE UKULELE

Into this world of oppositions and contradictions dropped two "Western" instruments: the Madeiran machete and rajão. Hawaiians almost immediately embraced and started rearranging them. Exact details and chronology of the process are unknown, but the instruments arrived in 1878 and the adaptation was completed by the mid–1880s.

What the Hawaiians did was to take the gut strings and tuning of the rajão and put them on the four-string machete, which became the ukulele, with reentrant guitar-style tuning (G C E A). In addition, they changed traditional European construction from using a spruce, pine, or similar top to building ukuleles completely out of indigenous Hawaiian koa, the wood historically associated with Hawaiian royalty, used for the thrones of kings.

The 5-string rajão was renamed the "taropatch" or "taropatch fiddle" and given the open-chord tuning of the machete, G D G B D, no longer reentrant.

These transformations coincided almost *exactly* with the appearance of Hawaiian slack-key guitar (with open tunings) and steel guitar (with open tunings and steel strings played with a steel bar). Around the turn of the 20th century or so, the taropatch began to transition into a four-course instrument with double strings tuned and played like a ukulele. However, memories of the original remain in the common Hawaiian slack-key tuning D G D G B D, which to this day is called "taropatch tuning."

Various colorful stories are told about how the ukulele got its name, some involving palace intrigue or defunct ancient instruments (such as the musical bow "*ukeke*"). But the most plausible is that the technique of rapidly strumming a machete while moving the hand between fingerboard and bridge looked like a "jumping flea," which is "ukulele" in Hawaiian.

King Kalakaua enthusiastically endorsed the new ukulele and became a close friend and promoter of Augusto Dias, even commissioning a uke of his own design and allowing Dias to adapt the royal coat of arms as a sign of authenticity on his instruments.

QUESTIONS OF IDENTITY

By the mid-1880s, photographers were capturing and disseminating images of both the uke and taropatch through popular mass-produced real-photo postcards and stereoviews. As early as the 1890s, ukuleles were being made and sold as souvenirs for the growing numbers of mainland tourists. The ukulele, along with grass skirts and leis, became a Hawaiian icon.

Hawaiian Islanders—both native and *haole*—were not the only ones struggling to redefine their identity at this time. An analogous process was going on—in a quite different context and on much greater scale—within mainland U.S. culture.

The evolving 19th century American identity played out against a background of revolutionary metamorphosis. The nation expanded westward to claim both coasts of the continent. People rushed into cities and built steel mills and shirt factories. They traveled cross-country by canals, railroads, and steamships, talking by telegraph and, later, telephone. Newly arrived citizens worked in the mills and factories speaking German, Gaelic, Italian, French, Yiddish, and Spanish. Wars were waged against Great Britain, Mexico, Spain, American Indians, and Secession.

ENTERTAINMENT LEAVES THE PLANTATION

One of the first steps toward a new American sense of self began by borrowing from African American culture. By the early 1800s Anglo Americans were playing 5-string banjos—an earlier fusion of African instruments and the Spanish guitar by slaves in the Caribbean. By the 1820s this had led to Blackface minstrelsy—performing on banjos in black make-up—and by 1843, at least, to the formalized minstrel show, considered by many to be one of the first truly American art forms.

Another step was taken when an American middle class emerged and began demanding more family-friendly forms of entertainment to supplant the what was the norm at the time: a liquor bar with a stage, for men only. Phineas T. Barnum opened his American Museum in New York in 1841, pioneering "sanitized" plays (no cussing or violence), live variety acts, and *curiosity* exhibits suitable for the wife and the kids. In 1865 Tony Pastor's Opera House debuted, moving the bar next door and allowing families to enjoy the show. This marked the beginning of American vaudeville which would spread this entertainment across the U.S.

Acts included minstrels, weightlifters, tight-rope walkers, "oddity" acts (such as Col. Thom Thumb), bicyclers, singers, dancers, anything out of the ordinary. As each new wave of immigrants appeared, they were quickly lampooned in stereotypical comedy sketches that ironically opened the door for ethnic entertainers to get on stage and satirize themselves, offering a fast track to the American Dream.

Increasingly, American audiences thronged to novel foreign entertainers. A very popular act touring the U.S. in 1867 was Prof. Risley's Imperial Japanese Troupe of acrobats and musicians, inspiring the rise of *Japonismé* in art and culture. One of the biggest phenomena of 1879 was a group called the Spanish Students, who—by means of a plethora of imitators—introduced America to the mandolin and inspired an explosion of string orchestras throughout the country.

FAREWELL TO THEE

Other important agents of cultural dispersion included World's Fairs and other international expositions. In addition to nationalistic exhibitions that showcased industrial innovation, trade prowess, and natural resources, these fairs and expos, most lasting several months, featured adjacent zones where attendees could enjoy "educational" or "culturally edifying" entertainment. Often this involved exotic ethnic peoples enlisted from far-flung colonies, or possessions displayed within reproductions of their native environments, underscoring the racial and cultural "superiority" of American and European civilization.

It was in these informal zones that Americans experienced their first Cracker Jacks, ice cream cones, hamburgers, Heinz ketchup and

Hawaiian girl playing a Dias ukulele.

mustard, Dr. Pepper, Pabst Blue Ribbon beer, Ferris Wheel ride, Little Egypt belly dance, and "primitive" African Hottentot, Filipino Igorot, and American Apache "villages."

Thus, it was on the Midway Plaisance attached to the World's Columbian Exposition in Chicago in 1893—just as the sugar barons were deposing Queen Liliuokalani in Honolulu—that Americans first encountered the Hawaiian ukulele and taropatch. Not far from the re-creation of a 26-building street in Cairo was the Kilauea Volcano Cyclorama (a 360-degree painting, with lava back-lit by newfangled electric lights). A large bandstand was erected in front where Hawaiian music and dance were performed. The Volcano Singers were the official band and included Nulhama "William" Aeko on guitar, ukulele, and taropatch. The Volcano Singers were popular but were greatly upstaged by "Kini Kapahu" (really Jennie Wilson), who worked the sidewalks with a uke and a seductive hula wiggle.

After the Columbian Exposition, Hawaiian music became a staple of American World's Fairs, notably in Portland, Oregon (1905), Seattle (1909), and others, with "Hawaii Days" featuring pineapples and Hawaiian music becoming commonplace. When the fairs closed, the musicians—including Jennie Wilson and members of the Volcano Singers—either joined the increasing number of touring Hawaiian troupes playing vaudeville circuits or settled in to enrich local music scenes.

One member of these touring groups was Iolai (July) Paka. He'd come to San Francisco in 1899 to cut some Edison cylinder recordings and married a part-Native American dancer from Michigan stage-named Toots, who donned a grass skirt and learned some hula moves. As Toots Paka's Hawaiian Troupe, they traveled the Orpheum vaudeville circuit, creating the standard model for subsequent Hawaiian ensembles (steel guitar, Spanish guitar, and ukulele). Hawaiian music slowly but steadily crept into the American consciousness.

THE UKULELE INVADES THE MAINLAND

Souvenir ukuleles trickled into the mainland from Hawaii beginning in the 1890s, and interest in Hawaiian music increased. The first noticeable sign of wider demand for ukuleles came in 1907, when the George G. Birkel Co. of Los Angeles began selling them. Later that year C.F. Martin became the first mainland guitar-maker to produce ukuleles, shipping a single lot of six units to the Bergstrom Music Co. in Honolulu.

By 1909 or 1910, Los Angeles guitar teacher Charles S. DeLano began studying the ukulele and steel guitar with the many Hawaiian musicians living there. By late 1908, there were more than 200 Hawaiian musicians working in the U.S., and virtually every upscale West Coast hotel considered Hawaiian orchestras essential for dining and dancing. Ukulele lessons were being advertised in L.A. and San Jose by 1912.

In 1909, the Oliver Ditson Co. of Boston published the first mainland tutorial, T.H. Robinson's *Method for the Ukulele (Hawaiian Guitar)*. In 1910, the Ditson affiliate in New York, Charles H. Ditson & Co., began promoting ukes as part of a group of instruments from remote countries around the world.

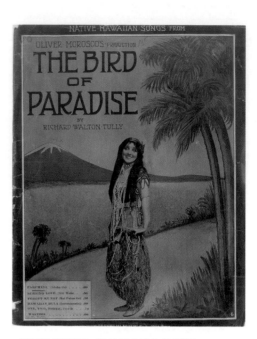

THE BIRD OF PARADISE

The growing sales of Hawaiian ukuleles got a major boost in 1912 with the success of the musical *Bird of Paradise*. Written by Richard Walton Tully, the play was an adaptation of Giacomo Puccini's popular opera *Madame Butterfly* (1904), with the same story (American sailor abandons native beauty when he returns "home"), but the locale changed from Japan to Hawaii. The show included Hawaiian songs—including Queen Liliuokalani's immortal "Aloha Oe"—played on Hawaiian and Spanish guitars (and also featured an erupting volcano!). "Hawaiian guitar" could mean steel guitar or ukulele because in the early days the term was sometimes applied interchangeably.

Bird of Paradise debuted on Broadway in January of 1912 with a limited success, but became a smash hit when it toured the U.S. and then was picked up by a host of local stock companies, playing continuously into the 1920s. Almost forgotten by modern theatrical historians, *Bird of Paradise* had an enormous impact in its day.

THE UKULELE TAKES OFF

The popularity of *Bird of Paradise* added fuel to the rise of the ukulele which, according to trade press accounts, really began to take off on the West Coast around 1913. That was the year that Manuel Nunes' son Leonardo, who'd worked in Honolulu for his father and uncle Julius, moved to Los Angeles and began providing ukuleles for George Birkel. By 1914 he was competing with his father, who was exporting ukes to the Southern California Music Co.

Sears, Roebuck & Co. also noticed that more people were playing the ukulele. Two mahogany ukuleles and a self-instruction book were offered for the first time in their Fall–Winter 1914 mail-order catalog. Anyone in America could now have a uke—almost certainly built by Harmony—delivered through the mail.

In 1915 the venerable guitar-maker C.F. Martin found itself financially strapped and returned to making ukuleles, a move that essentially saved the company from going out of business. Martin produced 12 ukuleles in 1915, 1,221 in 1916, and 3,446 in 1919.

By 1915 Honolulu ukulele makers included James N. Anahu, the Hawaiian Ukulele Co., Kinney & Mossman, Jonah Kumalae, M. Nunes & Sons, and Singer's Ukulele Manfuacturing Co. They were joined by the legendary Samuel K. Kamaka, Sr. the following year.

In 1915 more than 30,000 ukuleles were sold in California alone. Some mainland makers began marking their ukes as being "Made in Hawaii," which angered Hawaiian makers enough to petition American officials to make "Made in Hawaii U.S.A."—a legal trademark, and unauthorized use a punishable misdemeanor. This request failed, but in 1916 a "Tabu Made in Hawaii Trade Mark" began appearing on genuine Hawaiian ukes.

THE PANAMA-PACIFIC INTERNATIONAL EXHIBITION

This rising crescendo of interest in Hawaiian music and ukuleles climaxed between February and December of 1915 with the Panama-Pacific International Exposition (PPIE) held in San Francisco to celebrate the opening of the Panama Canal. Music and art were fundamental components of the PPIE's design. The Territory of Hawaii erected its own pavillion and there were numerous "Hawaii Days" where Exposition attendees might hear Keoki E. K. Awai's Royal Hawaiian Quartet, Henry Kailimai Quintette Club, Albert Vierra's Hawaiians, the DeLano Hawaiian Steel Guitar and Ukulele Sextette, Joseph Kekuku (probable inventor of steel guitar), Frank Ferera, and Pale K. Lua.

More than 18 million people visited San Francisco during the Expo and many left with a new taste for Hawaiian music and the ukulele. One of those was auto magnate Henry Ford, who hired Henry Kailimai and several others to move to Detroit, where they formed the Ford Hawaiians, cutting records and eventually performing on local radio.

For several years following the PPIE, Americans consumed Hawaiian music on phonograph records and in sheet music. Tin Pan Alley immediately jumped on the bandwagon cranking out countless "Hawaiian songs," most tunes—with titles like "The Honolulu Hicki Boola Boo" and "Yaaka Hula Hickey Dula"—composed by songwriters whose closest approach to Hawaii was likely Jersey City, or maybe Newark.

THE UKULELE GOES TO WAR

However, now that the ukulele had gone mainstream on the mainland, it was subject to broader influences. A big one came from Europe in the form of the Great War. In 1914 Europeans decided to reopen old wounds and

Hawaiian Village musicians at the Panama Pacific International Exposition, San Francisco, 1915.

1920s newspaper advertisement

gas. The United States limited its involvement to shipping armaments and singing "My Waikiki Ukulele Girl" until 1917, when the music changed to "Over There."

Accompanying the Doughboys to Europe were two new American art forms: jazz and Hawaiian music. The former was, like minstrelsy, another appropriation from African American culture; the latter featuring ukuleles. Both were played on the docks as troops left port and as morale-building entertainment for the soldiers in the trenches, either as shows sponsored by the YMCA or by commissioned military regiments.

The most famous of the U.S. Army jazz bands sent overseas was the 369th Infantry, the brass band led by the famous New York society orchestra leader (and music director for dancing idols Irene and Vernon Castle) James Reese Europe known as the "Harlem Hellfighters." But there

was also the Field Remount Squadron of the 331st Service Battalion, another renowned jazz outfit that played ukuleles and banjos.

Back home, music distributors and retailers launched campaigns urging families to send a uke or taropatch fiddle to the boys at war. Ukuleles became common companions in the cramped trench barracks. The Doughboys returned home to a world greatly changed from the drowsy waters from which the ukulele first arose. It was the Roaring Twenties. Beginning in 1920 women could vote . . . and no one could buy a (legal) drink. Flappers and speakeasies were poised to proliferate.

The ukulele's tenure in the trenches had scrubbed it free of its limitation to Hawaiian music and given it a carefree, modern caché. The ukulele became an ideal symbol for the fast-paced Jazz Age, a sure sign that its player was—or imagined he or she

was—a member of the "smart set." At least in terms of sheer numbers sold, this Jazz Age would also become the first Golden Age of Ukuleles.

UKULELES ON THE AIR

In addition to enfranchisement and prohibition, 1920 ushered in the age of radio broadcasting, the intimate nature of which was tailor-made for promoting the quiet-voiced ukulele. Early radio was a kind of Wild West, with no rules or precedents, and in essence it became a new vehicle for a more or less continuous vaudeville. It was no good for acrobats or bicycle acts, of course, but it was ideal for all sorts of musical and spoken word acts. Amidst the plethora of opera singers, orchestras, comedy acts, solo instrumentalists, radio dramas, yodelers, etc., you might also have heard the Schenectady Hawaiian Trio, Janey Hicky and the Mele Hawaiian Quartet,

Page Two   Hawaiian Guitars and Accessories

THE HAWAIIAN UKULELE AND TARO-PATCH FIDDLE
The Popular Novelties
Illustrations Show Comparative Size of Ukulele and Taro-Patch Fiddle

The Ukulele may be called the national instrument of the Hawaiian people. It is a diminutive form of guitar, developed in 1879, by the genius of Mr. Manuel Nunes, from the old "Taro - Patch Fiddle," an instrument which had been known in the Hawaiian Islands for more than a century. Mr. Nunes discovered the possibility and the means of producing from the tiny guitar shaped instrument a good volume of tone, and also succeeded in imparting to it a characteristic quality of timbre perfectly in keeping with the weird, fascinating native music.

This clever invention of Mr. Nunes was taken up with greatest enthusiasm by all classes of Hawaiian society. Kalakaua, who was then king, and his wife, the late Queen Kapiolani, together with princes and princesses of

Ukulele

Taro-Patch Fiddle

Lyon & Healy ukulele and taropatch from the 1918 catalog.

or Wiki Bird and Anita Ransom (on ukulele). Or you might have heard former vaudevillian and uke player Wendell Hall—the "Red-Headed Music Maker" who had a hit with "It Ain't Gonna Rain No Mo." Or another former carnival worker and vaudevillian named Cliff Edwards—stage-name Ukulele Ike—who strummed jazz rhythms and was among the first to sing jazz scat (he later became the unforgettable voice of Disney's Jiminy Cricket). Or May Singhi Breen, "The Ukulele Lady." Or Johnny Marvin, "The Ukulele Ace." Or Roy Smeck, "The Wizard of the Strings."

THE UKULELE FAMILY EXPANDS

With new momentum provided by radio, in 1922 ukulele accompaniments began to be routinely added to sheet music releases by Tin Pan Alley music publishers. Virtually every pop song for the next few years featured ukulele chord diagrams over the standard notation for voice and piano.

Also in 1922, the standard, or soprano, ukulele began to get some siblings. Lyon & Healy's 1922–23 catalog featured a "tenor ukulele," although terminology was loose back then, so at 24-1/2 inches it isn't clear if this was a large concert or small tenor uke.

As we have seen, around the turn of the century the taropatch fiddle, a remade rajāo, began transitioning from a 5-string instrument to a four-course, double-strung instrument tuned like a ukulele. In 1925 C.F. Martin removed one string from each course to create a 4-string taropatch. Slightly larger than a soprano ukulele, this 4-string taropatch was first called a "tenor ukulele" (perhaps taking its cue from L&H), changed to "concert ukulele" in September, perhaps in response to the introduction of a "concert ukulele" by Schulz & Moenning (Chicago) at almost the very same time.

A certain amount of clarity was given to the marketplace in 1926 when the National Association of Musical Instrument and Accessories Manufacturers codified specifications for stringed instruments. A soprano ukulele should have a string length of 13 inches to 13-3/4 inches. A concert ukulele should measure 13-3/4 inches to 15-1/2 inches. A tenor ukulele should have a 14-1/2-inch to 15-3/4-inch scale.

However, as seen in the 1927 catalog of Buegeleisen & Jacobson, the major New York City distributor, this trio of ukuleles had other brothers and sisters, including "baby ukuleles" (probably a sopranino) and "bass ukuleles," although, again, just exactly what that was is uncertain and probably *not* the modern bass ukulele. Gibson introduced its first tenor ukulele in 1928, described as a "Grand Concert Ukulele."

BOOM AND BUST

The peak of Roaring Twenties ukulele-mania occurred in 1925–26, with 1925 showing a 100-percent increase in sales over 1924. Demand was so great that string instrument makers could not keep up. One industry expert estimated that 4,000,000 ukuleles were sold in 1925, the year of Martin's greatest ukulele production, when it made a whopping 14,532 ukuleles. Jay Kraus of Harmony reported that the company built 4,000 to 5,000 ukuleles a week in 1926. One Chicago shop, Rialto Music House, sold 3,000 ukuleles in three months at the beginning of 1926. In 1927, Lyon & Healy boasted that it could make several hundred ukuleles a day. Practically every issue of the trade press enthused about ukuleles and ukulele-banjos. Interest in ukuleles was so great that the Albert J. Wasserman Co. of Wheeling, West Virginia, introduced an attachment for pianos that replicated the sound of a ukulele! Makers of other kinds of instruments got into the game, glutting the market with ridiculously cheap ukuleles.

Almost inevitably, in late 1926 ukuleles hit the proverbial brick wall. Martin uke production dropped to 9,749 in 1926, to 5,124 in 1927, and to 3,400 in

Godfrey-endorsed ukes

1928. It seems that everyone who was going to play a ukulele already had one . . . or two . . . or three.

With C.F. Martin selling nearly 15,000 ukuleles in 1925, clearly some people were taking ukuleles seriously. In 1926, a mahogany Martin Style 1 soprano cost $14 and the koa Style 5K cost $55 (Martin's top-of-the-line 000-45 guitar cost $175). The average factory worker earned about $25 a week back then. But by the Great Depression ukuleles had large-

ly become novelty items, shaped like airplanes (the Aero-Uke) or stenciled with images of Betty Boop.

Ukuleles would not recover any widespread popularity until after World War II. When they finally did, they were still considered little more than novelties, like before the war. Their return to grace would be thanks to a showman who participated in the serious ukulele boom of the early 1920s and a new entertainment medium, television.

THE OL' REDHEAD

In 1920—just as the ukulele was transitioning from being an exclusively Hawaiian property to belonging to everyone—a young man lied about his age and joined the Navy. Born in 1903, Arthur Godfrey served as a Navy radio operator from 1920–24. While in training at Great Lakes Naval Station in Illinois, he was taught to play ukulele by a fellow recruit from Maui. During a subsequent stint with the U.S. Coast Guard, in 1929 he appeared on a Baltimore radio station as an amateur tenor banjo and ukulele player. He got his own radio show in 1930. By 1941 he was broadcasting in New York City and in December of 1948 appeared on his first television show, *Arthur Godfrey's Talent Scouts*, followed in January 1949 by *Arthur Godfrey and His Friends*. The ukulele became a signature feature of Godfrey's act.

Arthur Godfrey strumming his uke on radio and television revived interest in the ukulele for the first time in more than a decade. However, most of this involved not "real" ukuleles, but plastic toy ukuleles—such as Mattel's polystyrene Uke-A-Doodle and several knock-off competitors introduced in 1947—for kids. And there was a huge, growing audience of kids with the postwar Baby Boom.

MAESTRO MACCAFERRI'S MASTRO

The plastic toys may have contributed some influence, but Godfrey made a bigger impact the day he strummed an actually playable Islander ukulele made of Dow Styron plastic on TV. The next day, Mario Maccaferri's phone didn't stop ringing and he would go on to produce 9 million plastic ukuleles before he closed up shop in 1969.

Catalog offerings from Harmony, 1958.

Maccaferri, a concert classical guitarist who designed the distinctive Selmer guitars associated with Django Reinhardt in the early 1930s, invented the plastic reed favored by Benny Goodman in 1939. When World War II broke out, he got a government contract to provide reeds for military bands. That qualified as "war material," so he didn't have to build anything else. It also allowed him to obtain injection molding equipment. Maccaferri worked with Dow Chemical to develop a formulation that could not only be infinitely colored, it could be tuned like a fine tonewood. So, while Maccaferri's ukuleles—and later guitars and other instruments—were marketed as toys, they were built with considerable handwork, included sophisticated features, and sounded as good as many of the wood ukuleles that resumed production at this time.

Nevertheless, the new ukulele boom yielded little more than beginner instruments for Baby Boomers. Endless anecdotes are told of famous rock stars who got their starts on a ukulele before graduating to a guitar, including Jimi Hendrix, Johnny Winter, George Benson, Ian Anderson, Peter Frampton, Neil Young, and, while never a star, yours truly.

ON THE GOOD SHIP LOLLIPOP

On January 22, 1968, ukuleles, which by then were mostly just a fond youthful memory, turned into a liv-

ing nightmare when Tiny Tim strolled onto the set of *Rowan and Martin's Laugh-In* TV show, accompanying himself singing, in a piercing falsetto, "On the Good Ship Lollipop" and "Tiptoe Through the Tulips." Some consider this the ukulele's nadir, though it did bring a renewed visibility to the instrument.

You can only go up from Tiny Tim! The ukulele was saved from extinction by the resurgence of interest in native Hawaiian culture within its homeland. Led by the ukulele virtu-

oso Eddie Kamae and slack-key guitar ace Gabby Pahinui, this included Hawaiian music. In 1971, historian George Hanahele started the Hawaiian Music Foundation to preserve and promote native music. That same year, Sunday Manoa released the revolutionary album *Guava Jam*, essentially "Hawaiian fusion." And 1971 also saw the beginning of the Honolulu Parks and Recreation's annual ukulele festival, which continues to this day as one of the most important events in the ukulele universe.

1960 Harmony Roy Smeck   1968 Aloha Duke Kahanamoku

THE THIRD WAVE

But unlike previous Hawaiian musical movements, the Hawaiian Renaissance had only minimal effect on the mainland. However, beginning in the early 1990s, the long-neglected ukulele began to attract a kind of nostalgic interest in the United States and around the world, fueled in no small part by the efforts of Jim Beloff and others, not to mention the burgeoning internet. Beloff even revived the plastic ukulele, introducing the Fluke in 1999. This awareness was abetted by the appearance of brilliant young fingerstyle players such as Jake Shimabukuro, who launched his solo concert career in 2001, greatly expanding the possibilities of the ukulele. By the early 2000s, music stores began sponsoring ukulele clubs and camps. This revival is often called the "Third Wave" and continues to this day.

Among the many effects of the Third Wave were the return of ukulele making to Hawaii, the explosion of high-end handmade ukuleles, and the ready availability of high-quality entry-level instruments made primarily in Asia.

THE SECOND GOLDEN AGE

In Hawaii, the only major ukulele maker to survive into the modern era was the shop of Samuel Kamaka, Sr. (founded 1916). Just a few of the better-known new custom ukulele workshops include KoAloha, Kanile'a, Ko'olou, Koa Works, Moore Bettah, Kula Custom Ukes, and Pahu Kani. Today there are around 25 custom ukulele makers in Hawaii alone.

As in Hawaii, the mainland also experienced a great increase in custom ukulele makers with shops concentrating heavily, though not entirely, along the coasts and in the Midwest. Some of these—such as DaSilva, Kinnard, Kimo, Mya-Moe, Graziano, Hoffmann, and G-String—specialize in ukuleles. Other luthiers—such as Gary Zimnicki, Jay Lichty, Kevin Mason, and Les Stansell—are primarily or also guitar-makers but are famous for their ukes, too.

The Third Wave also caught the attention of premium guitar-making companies who began building premium ukuleles, including the venerable C.F. Martin and boutique makers such as Collings, Larrivée, Turner, and others.

Custom, hand-made ukuleles are not exclusive to the United States. The range is suggested by this small sampling: Antica Ukulereria (Verona, Italy), Argapa (Stockholm, Sweden), Barron River (Cairns, Australia), Cocobolo (Nicaragua), Ferangeli (Cebu, Philippines), Grenosi (Vienna, Austria), and Pete Howlett, (Gwynedd, UK).

These are not your grandfather's ukuleles! They are all custom-built with fine woods and often elaborate inlays and trim. A basic model will cost just under $1,000, while a deluxe custom uke may cost up to $5,000 or more; sometimes a *lot* more! Compare that to the most expensive Martin in 1926 that set you back $55, or about two weeks' wages.

GO EAST YOUNG MAN

The Third Wave luckily coincided with the rise in Asian manufacturers outside of Japan and Korea. The principal source for Asian ukuleles is China, but there are factories in Indonesia, Taiwan, and Vietnam, as well. Generally speaking, these companies supply beginner to mid-level ukuleles, often of surprisingly good quality. You may encounter one of these when you buy a ukulele with a popular guitar name, such as Aria, Applause, Córdoba, Epiphone, Fender, Gretsch, Ibanez, National, Oscar Schmidt, and Ovation. Or you are likely to find them among popular ukulele brands such as Lanikai, Kala, Nalu, Enya, and others.

The jumping flea has been dancing now for 140 years. The Third Wave has already been going strong for almost three decades and shows no sign of abating. Vintage ukulele prices continue to rise, and there have never been so many new choices at whatever level you can—or choose to—participate. History may deal the ukulele a future hand with another Tiny Tim, but for now, have fun pulling out your ukulele to strum along to a swaying hula or an energetic Charleston or *any* other style that suits you.

One thing the Third Wave has shown conclusively is that ukulele has no limits! *u*

WHEN UKES ALONE AREN'T ENOUGH

Balance your strummables with ukulele-themed collectibles

BY JUMPIN' JIM BELOFF

The collecting fever known as known as Ukulele Acquisition Syndrome (or UAS) can also extend beyond, well . . . ukuleles. For some uke aficionados it can spread to all sorts of categories of collecting. This can include paper treasures like vintage sheet music, songbooks, magazine covers, greeting cards, advertising, menus, and photos, and move on to bulkier items like vintage hula nodders, Hawaiian shirts, and even pineapple crates. Pretty much anything with an image of a ukulele or just the word itself is a candidate for the archives.

One thing I learned early on in my collecting days was that the ukulele was so accepted in its first two waves of popularity that it found its way into every nook and cranny of mainstream culture. In fact, during one heyday, it was not uncommon to find movie stills with cast members cavorting with ukuleles, while never touching one in the actual film. What this bit of

false advertising suggests is that the ukulele had become a form of visual shorthand, implying that the film was a comedy, had songs in it, was based in Hawaii, or even all three at once.

The ukulele was also a central piece of visual vocabulary during the golden age of Hawaiian tourism. The classic image of someone playing the ukulele underneath a palm tree was employed in countless ways to help sell a romantic and exotic destination. In the late 1930s, when Matson cruise ships were traveling regularly between California and Hawaii, the dinner menus featured a series of five different covers by California illustrator Frank McIntosh. The menu cover on the final night before arriving in Hawaii featured a multicolored illustration of a ukulele surrounded by tropical fruits and flowers. It's still relatively easy to find the original menus today because so many passengers chose to save them.

When I found a Martin tenor ukulele in 1992 at the Rose Bowl Flea

Market in Pasadena, California, it lit a fire that stills burns bright today. Over the years, my wife Liz and I have enjoyed countless hours scouring flea markets, antique shows, and estate sales for ukulele-related items. We've justified this pursuit by using many of the images in our books, including *The Ukulele: A Visual History* and our *Jumpin' Jim's* series of ukulele songbooks. For those who know our *Daily Ukulele* songbooks, virtually all of the photographs of people holding ukuleles were found by combing through old boxes of photos at paper shows or on eBay. As Liz was laying out the book she would often wonder if the people in these old photos would ever be recognized. Lately it's begun to happen. So far, players in three of the photos have been identified.

Before I close, I'd like to give a shoutout to one of the great collectors of ukulele ephemera. At the early uke fests of the current third wave, Bob Cuoco would display huge notebooks full of paper ephemera that he had collected over the years. One notebook in particular featured hundreds of vintage uke-themed postcards. Eventually, he reached a point where he no longer wanted to care for the collection and offered to sell much of the archive to us. Our UAS kicked in and we jumped at the chance to merge his collection with ours. And now, we're sharing some of it here. I like to tell people to be careful what you find at flea markets. It can change your life! So be warned, viewing some of these items might just ignite your own UAS. Happy hunting!

POSTCARDS & PHOTOS

Vintage postcards and
photos featuring people with
their ukuleles can be found at
paper shows and on eBay.

Poncie Ponce
"HAWAIIAN EYE"
WKRC-TV ● CHANNEL 12

INSTRUMENT ADS
Another category of ephemera
is vintage ads for ukuleles.

HAWAIIANA
A menu from
the Matson
cruise lines,
and a Dole
pineapple crate
are examples
of some of the
Island-related
treasures in our
collection.

MAGAZINES, VALENTINES, ADS

Over the years, the ukulele has been used regularly as a prop on magazine covers, valentines, and in advertisements.

ART UKULELES

This Islander plastic ukulele was a gift from Maria Maccaferri, wife of Mario Maccaferri, who designed and manufactured the Islander and other plastic musical instruments in the 1950s and 1960s. The painted illustration was by Carrie Singhi, sister of May Singhi Breen, arranger of many ukulele songbooks from the 1920s and later.

METHOD BOOKS & SHEET MUSIC

There have been dozens of songs published with "ukulele" in the title. The sheet music to these songs often features beautiful and dramatic covers. We also collect sheet music that shows someone playing a ukulele on the cover.

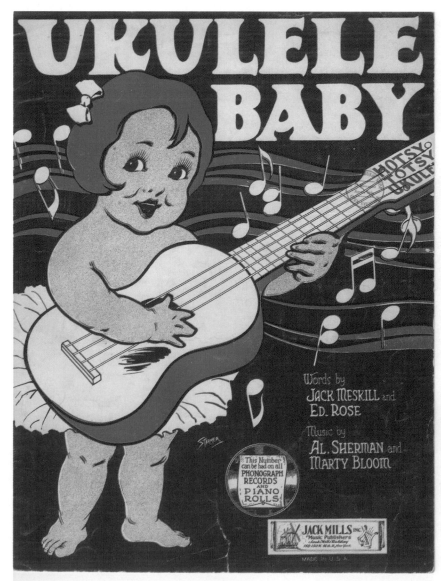

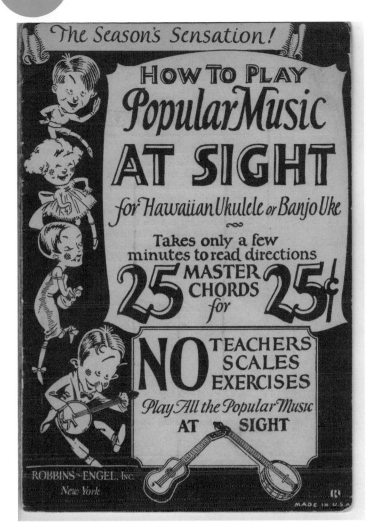

FROM SUBLIME TO SILLY

A small collection of historic and unusual ukes

Given the ukulele's incredible rise in popularity in recent times, it's not surprising that they've become items to collect as much as to play. It can start innocently enough: You get one, then you get another, then you realize that cool vintage ukes are still reasonably affordable. Even better, they're small, so storing a growing collection isn't a challenge. And ukes are just plain fun; as you can see here, many have unusual designs and pretty woods.

Most of the ukes shown here belong to Elderly Instruments' founder Stan Werbin, who is no stranger to vintage instruments. Werbin—who remembers selling old Martin ukes in his store for $25, "because nobody wanted them" in the 1970s—was bitten by the uke bug early on, buying entire collections and keeping quite a few for his personal enjoyment. "You can fit ten ukes in the space of one guitar," he says, explaining that he never had the space to keep a lot of guitars at his house.

The majority of the ukes featured here are from the "ukulele craze" of the 1920s and '30s, though some are from earlier or later years. They represent a cross-section of important brands, lesser-known pioneers, and plain old cornball fun. Some are the only ukes of their kind, while others were produced en masse.

We take no responsibility if what you see here inspires you to start searching out unique ukes yourself, but be warned that few folks can stop at one! —*Teja Gerken*

1 Made by Stromberg-Voisinet (a predecessor to Kay), the airplane-inspired Aero Uke is one of the most unusual designs ever conceived. Note the propeller-shape in the front of the body, and the "rudder" mounted to the face of the headstock.

2 Jonah Kumalae was one of the first important Hawaiian uke builders. Initially working by himself, he eventually ran a small production shop in Honolulu. This all-koa instrument from about 1920 is an early example of his work.

3 A Maestro Beatles uke made of polystyrene. Essentially a decorated version of the plastic Maccaferri Islander ukes, this special model was available in the mid-1960s.

4 Luthier Samuel Kaialiilii Kamaka had the idea of using a pineapple shape for his ukuleles' bodies back in 1916. The design was a huge success, and he received a patent for it in 1928. This example is made from koa and features the pineapple's texture and leaves painted into the wood. Kamaka was, of course, the founder of the famous and successful company that still bears his family name more than 100 years after its founding.

5 Manufactured by the Harmony Company, this late '20s or early '30s birch uke features images from the popular comic strip *Harold Teen*, which ran in newspapers from 1919 to 1959, and was the first major strip to center on an adolescent character.

6 Built sometime in the 1930s, this Gibson uke is clearly a custom creation, with scenes of Venice not only painted onto its mahogany body, but even between frets on the ivoroid fingerboard.

2

3

4

5

6

'UKULELE LADY'
1920s Custom Martin 5M

We don't know whether 1920s uke star May Singhi Breen ordered this custom soprano uke herself or it was a gift. But with her nickname, "Ukulele Lady," inlaid on the fingerboard and her given name—as well as the call letters of the New York NBC radio station where she was frequently featured—adorning the headstock, there is no doubt that it is a personalized instrument that came out of whatever "custom shop" Martin had in those days. True to the 5M style, the instrument is built with beautifully figured mahogany (top, back, and sides) and features abalone around the body and a multilayer abalone rosette. This is from the collection Elderly Instruments' Stan Werbin.
—Teja Gerken

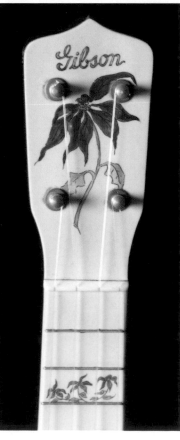

A RARE FLOWER
A puzzling ca. 1930 Gibson
Poinsettia

Why Gibson chose to festoon an ukulele with poinsettias is anyone's guess, but it's hard to argue with the striking results of this rare instrument. Only a handful of the custom-ordered poinsettias are known today and each seems to have unique features. The top-of-the-line Uke-3 production model had a mahogany body and ivoroid fingerboard, with poinsettias painted on the top, back, sides, fingerboard, and front and back of the headstock. It first appeared Gibson's 1927–28 catalog and was available into the early 1930s.
—Greg Olwell

A KOA CLASSIC
Circa 1920 Weissenborn Concert

After spending several years repairing pianos and violins in New York City (from around 1902 to 1910), German immigrant Hermann Weissenborn (1863–1937) set up shop in Los Angeles, where he began building stringed instruments. In adapting the principles of hollow-neck guitar design from Norwegian Chris J. Knutsen, Wessenborn's refined vision of hollow-neck Hawaiian guitars produced a full, rich tone favored by Hawaiian guitar players in the early part of the 20th century. He also made a small number of highly coveted ukuleles like this early concert-size koa model with a "V" pattern in the book-matched back. This instrument is very loud and sweet sounding   —*Derek See*

PURE GOLD
A top-of-the-line Style E Kumalae

The great Hawaiian luthier Jonah Kumalae (1875–1940) famously won a Gold Award at San Francisco's Panama Pacific International Exhibition in 1915. Following that, Kumalae's uke production skyrocketed. At its peak, Kumalae and his small, family-run business were making as many as 500 or more ukes every month. According to a 1917 catalog, the company's top-of-the-line Style E soprano sold for $18 and featured "the finest grade of handsome old seasoned koa, inlaid neck and body, extra heavy." It also boasted a "banjo-style peghead" and a fancy rope pattern on the neck and top edge. This instrument was a family heirloom that once belonged to my wife's Honolulu-born grandfather, Haruto Umemoto, who most likely gained possession of it in 1926 or 1927—possibly as a parting gift before he left for college on the mainland.
—*Marc Greilsamer*

ONLINE RESOURCE GUIDE

Uke Manufacturers, Builders & Retailers

While this is by no means a complete list of the many companies and people that are making and selling ukuleles, strings, and other accessories, it will certainly give you an idea of the range of instruments and products out there. And although we have limited this list to merchants who sell online, keep in mind your local independent music store will likely have ukes and accessories, too! And if you're just in the mood to *look* at beautiful ukuleles, an entertaining rabbit hole to go down is sampling the custom wares in the "Builders" section. Happy hunting!   —*Blair Jackson*

Manufacturers

Amahi Ukuleles amahiukuleles.com
Breedlove breedlovemusic.com/instruments/ukuleles
C.F. Martin & Co.   martinguitar.com/guitars/ukulele
Córdoba Guitars cordobaguitars.com/ukuleles
Deering Banjo Co. deeringbanjos.com/collections/goodtime-banjo-ukuleles
Duke Banjo Ukuleles dukeuke.com
Eastman Guitars eastmanguitars.com/other_fretted
Enya Music enya-music.com
Farida faridausa.com/collections/farida-ukuleles
Fender Musical Instruments shop.fender.com/en-US/ukuleles
Gold Tone Music Group goldtonemusicgroup.com
Ibanez ibanez.com/usa/products/model/ukulele
Kala Brand Music Co. kalabrand.com
Kamaka Ukulele kamakahawaii.com
Kanile'a 'Ukulele kanileaukulele.com
KoAloha koaloha.com
Kremona Trade, Inc. kremonausa.com
Lanikai Ukuleles lanikaiukuleles.com
Luna Ukuleles (Armadillo Enterprises) lunaguitars.com/ukuleles
Magic Fluke magicfluke.com
Ohana Music ohana-music.com
Opal Instruments opalinstruments.com/ukuleles
Orangewood Guitars orangewoodguitars.com/collections/marina-collection
Ortega Guitars ortegaguitars.com
Romero Creations romerocreations.com
Saga Musical Instruments sagamusic.com
Strong Wind Musical Instrument Co., Ltd.   strong-wind.com
Takumi Ukulele Company takumiukulele.com

Builders

Ana'ole
anaoleukulele.com

Beansprout Musical Instruments
thebeansprout.com

Boulder Creek Guitars
bouldercreekguitars.com/riptide-ukuleles

Collings Guitars
collingsguitars.com/custom-gallery/ukuleles

DaSilva Ukulele Co.
ukemaker.com

DeVine Guitars and Ukuleles
devineguitars.com

Tony Graziano Ukuleles
grazianoukuleles.com

Grimes Guitars
grimesguitars.com

Joe Green Ukulele
joegreenukulele.com

Imua Ukuleles
imuabrand.com

Kimo Ukulele
kimoukulele.com

Ko'olau Guitar and Ukulele Co.
koolauukulele.com

Lichty Guitars and Ukuleles
lichtyguitars.com

Little River Ukuleles
littleriverukuleles.com

Mele Ukulele Maui
shopmeleukulele.com

Moore Bettah Ukuleles
moorebettahukes.com

Mya-Moe Ukuleles
myamoeukuleles.com

Oceana Ukuleles
oceanaukuleles.com

Petros Ukuleles
petrosukuleles.com

Talsma String Instruments
davetalsma.com/custom-ukuleles

Rick Turner
rickturnerguitars.com/ukuleles

Uke Republic (custom curators)
ukerepublic.com

Gary Zimnicki
zimnicki.com/instruments/ukulele

Strings & Accessories

Aquila Strings aquilacorde.com/en/modern-music
C.F. Martin & Co. martinguitar.com/1833-shop/ukulele/c-24/p-1324
Crossrock Case Co. crossrockcase.com
D'Addario & Company daddario.com
Ernie Ball Inc. ernieball.com
GHS Strings ghsstrings.com
Graph Tech Guitar Labs graphtech.com
The Hug Strap thehugstrap.com
Just Strings juststrings.com/ukulele.html
Korg USA korg.com/us/products/tuners
Kyser Musical Products kysermusical.com
Luthier Music luthiermusic.com
Mick's Picks mickspicks.com
Music Nomad (equipment care) musicnomadcare.com
Oasis (humidifiers) oasishumidifiers.com
Peterson Tuners petersontuners.com
Shubb Capos shubb.com
Strings By Mail stringsbymail.com/ukulele-strings-684
TKL (cases) tkl.com/products?categories=ukulclc

Retailers
(Nearly all of these companies carry both instruments and accessories)

Empire Music empiremusic.net
Funky Frets funkyfrets.com/brands/ukuleles
Guitar Center guitarcenter.com/Ukuleles.gc
Reverb reverb.com
Sam Ash Music Stores samash.com
The Strum Shop thestrumshop.com
Sweetwater sweetwater.com/c1053—Ukuleles
Uke Life Co. ukelifeco.com
The Uke Room theukeroom.com
Ukulele Friend ukulelefriend.com/uke-store
The Ukulele Site theukulelesite.com

CONTRIBUTORS

JIM BELOFF is a highly respected and prolific musician, performer, songwriter, composer, producer, and publisher who has been active in the ukulele scene worldwide since the early 1990s. He and his wife, Liz, run Flea Market Music (fleamarketmusic.com), selling a wide variety of recordings, songbooks, and videos.

CRAIG CHEE and **SARAH MAISEL** are world-renowned ukulele performers and instructors. They have spent the last eight years traveling the world together, sharing the joy of this instrument. Both are known for their ukulele retreats, cruises, and online school with ArtistWorks. craigandsarah.com

DOUGLAS REYNOLDS is president of PlayUke.net and is the founder of the Reno and Palm Springs ukulele festivals. He runs the ukulele department at Play Your Own Music in Carson City, Nevada. A life-long guitarist, he fell prey to the call of the ukulele in 2005.

DAVE SIGMAN is a luthier and inlay artist who runs Little River Ukuleles (littleriverukuleles.com), formerly out of Mendocino County, California, but now based on the Big Island of Hawaii.

Although she didn't have a ukulele in her hand, **HEIDI SWEDBERG** was born in Hawaii. Her first uke came to her via the Easter Bunny, and she continues to share her childish delight with the little instrument with people of all ages at festivals and in classrooms around the world.

AARON KEIM is a luthier at Beansprout Musical Instruments (thebeansprout.com) and also a busy educator, historian, writer, and performer. He performs with his wife, Nicole, in the Quiet American.

MICHAEL WRIGHT is a historian and journalist who has played and collected guitars since he began playing ukulele in 1952. He's been a columnist for *Vintage Guitar* since 1991, has published all or part of more than 15 books on guitar history, contributes to Oxford's *Grove Dictionary of Music*, and is a regular presenter to the Annual Banjo Gathering.

MIM has been setting up and selling ukuleles since 2010. Her shop is nestled in the hollow of Slate Mountain in Floyd, Virginia. She also loves to perform, teach, and emcee open mics at ukulele festivals as Mim's Ukulele Sideshow. MimsUkes.com

GREG OLWELL has been a ukulele evangelist since first discovering its joys in the '90s. He is also a former editor of *Ukulele* and a regular contributor since its launch.

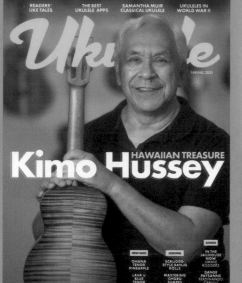
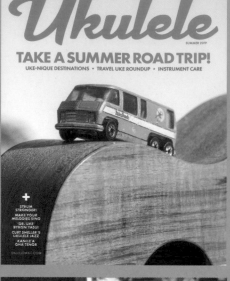
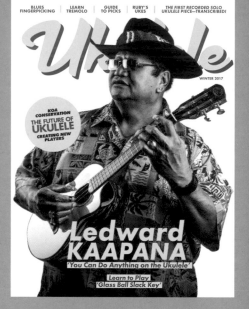
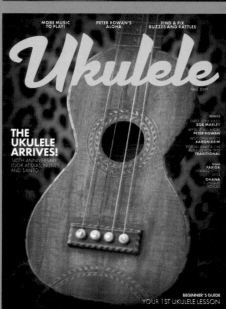